Jeremy Masding
Emil Ivanov

Leading
Without
Winging It

A Guide To
Navigating 30 Timeless
Leadership Issues

ISBN:
9798224087198   (Print Edition)
9798223757047   (eBook Edition)

First Published as an eBook in 2023 by Top Management Institute.

www.leadingwithoutwingingit.com

TABLE OF CONTENTS

ABOUT US

All successful partnerships thrive on differences – of opinions, approaches and personalities. It is those differences that have enabled us to debate, to disagree, to agree and, ultimately, to develop a partnership that brings out the best in us. We have worked together for over 25 years with a shared passion for learning, developing, and creating value.

Jeremy Masding has a deep passion for leading and making a difference whilst wanting to work with (and develop) good people to be the best they can be.

Jeremy is motivated by the difficult job, the impossible task, or the broken business that needs mending. Jeremy does not enjoy 'business as usual' as such. He wants to work with good people to fix, to build and to embed the highest standards of thinking and doing. He takes enormous pride in building something sustainable, greater than the sum of its parts and that has real impact.

In addition, Jeremy is a passionate believer in the power of management science and disciplined approaches to work. He believes that 'shoddy thinking leads to shoddy doing' so will drive people hard to find the best set of facts, create the best insights, debate the best alternatives, use the best rules for decision-making, and select the value-maximising alternative course of action. He will then hold colleagues to account for delivering on commitments to time, cost, and quality. Jeremy expects a lot from people, demands the highest standards, and pursues value creation relentlessly. At the same time, he believes this should be done in a way that allows colleagues to develop and live up to their fullest potential.

When reflecting on the motivations behind co-authoring this book, Jeremy observed:

"I understand there are many, many different definitions of leadership but the one I use the most is that 'leadership is giving your colleagues a choice about whether to be part of the business or not'. As such, I wanted to be wholly transparent (and grounded) in explaining our core beliefs and being clear about how we run a business.

I wanted to offer a clear, practical, and actionable toolkit to help leaders of all experience levels be the best they can. In this regard, I am very conscious of the rise of stakeholder capitalism and ancillary schools of thought. I wanted the book to offer a different perspective, a modern view of shareholder capitalism, if you will, that protects the primacy of equity capital whilst thinking deeply about how this should work in practice without widespread collateral damage. If this book challenges people to think, offers an alternative way of working or questions the emerging status quo, then mission accomplished".

Emil Ivanov is reflective, thoughtful, inquisitive, caring, and smart. He is comfortable strategizing, building, implementing, influencing, and subtly making a difference. Emil has an academic mind and is constantly thinking about and testing new ideas and concepts. He has always been deeply interested in management science, i.e., how companies work and how people behave in the workplace – covering the complete spectrum from the rational to the emotional side of business and from visions to management systems. He understands clearly how the rational and emotional interconnect and is skilled in developing and embedding the required toolkits that enable other people to think and do better.

Emil is a deep thinker who thrives on detail, insight and solving problems. His active intellect is accompanied by creativity and action. He can mix 'thinking and doing' in equal measure – this is a rare superpower.

In addition, Emil is fascinated by why people do what they do, especially if it does not serve them positively in the long-term. He is a keen student of human behaviour – with a strong ability to identify narcissistic and self-defeating behaviour. He is motivated by collaboration and teamwork underpinned by a robust management system. Consequently, Emil also understands adeptly how to recruit, select, and develop top talent.

When reflecting on the motivations behind the co-authoring this book, Emil observed:

"I have always been driven by understanding the inner workings of business, leading, managing, and interacting with people. I wanted to share my learnings and experiences in the simplest of terms – the big leadership issues, the principles to be applied in solving the issues, the positive actions that can be taken towards that end, and the pitfalls to be avoided.

If this book helps people make better decisions, take the right actions, and, critically, do so in a way that is underpinned by personal integrity, compassionate candour and without a blinding ego, then I have achieved successfully what I set out to do."

In summary, our complementary characteristics have contributed to building a successful track record of value creation for many businesses over the years. However, it is the 'medals and scars' picked up from real-life experiences that initially motivated us to co-write this book. Having observed, experimented, failed, and succeeded many times in the past, we know well what 'good' and 'bad' looks like in terms of setting strategy, engaging colleagues, building supporting systems and processes, measuring performance, and holding each other (and colleagues) to account.

As co-authors, we do hope this book will help you be the best you can be and maximise your leadership potential.

JEREMY MASDING & EMIL IVANOV

INTRODUCTION

We were sitting in Dublin Airport waiting for a flight. With time on our hands, we followed the standard agenda – food, drink, shopping, chatting. It was while scanning the shelves of the bookshops that the idea for this book came to us. The business section bookshelves were predominantly filled with leadership books written either autobiographically with limited practical advice or by academics peddling the latest theory.

It occurred to us that there was a gap in the market for a book written by those with broad and deep leadership experience, those with medals and scars, who could offer a perspective on how to approach some of the persistent issues that come with the privilege of leading.

In this book, we offer a perspective on perennial leadership issues based on strong practical and experiential foundations. We have learnt through experience (good and bad) and are confident that we offer a tried, tested, and practical approach.

We offer the reader a construct to lead and influence an organisation and to maximise sustainable value for the owners (shareholders), which we argue must always be the Governing Objective of any shareholder-owned business despite all the noise of 'stakeholder capitalism'. We hope to give the reader a practical framework of principles and actions, not a theoretical paradigm. We have attempted to cover each topic at a sufficient level to make it practical and come alive.

Our approach to the perennial leadership issues and the construct we offer to our readers reduces any chances of 'winging it', as team members will see straight through this approach to leadership at any level of the organisation. We know being a leader means that there is nowhere to hide. Everything you do is out in the open. You can try winging it, but sooner or later, you will be found out.

We hope to provoke the reader to think and challenge our perspectives and then apply the appropriate disciplines for their organisations. Indeed, we are adamant that good discipline in both thinking and doing is a minimum standard for any organisation – from entrepreneurial to large corporate. We would go so far as to say that good discipline is a source of competitive advantage.

Some of the principles in this book rely on the seminal works of others – most notably *The Value Imperative* by James M. McTaggart, Peter Kontes, and Michael C. Mankins; *Radical Candor* by Kim Scott; and *WHO: The A Method for Hiring* by Geoff Smart and Randy Street. Of course, there are many leadership books that push the boundaries of management science and practice; however, in our experience, the above texts are the best examples. They offer timeless advice that we have tested rigorously, time and again.

As a principle, we have shied away from 'management speak' or the technical language of our industry, banking, because we would like for the principles and frameworks in this book to be available to the largest possible audience – from management students to CEOs, Chairpersons, and everyone else in-between. If you are not a CEO, do not worry. Studying these perennial leadership questions will help you put yourself in the shoes of a CEO and will prepare you for a leadership role in your company.

Many of the topics in this book rely on understanding human nature; for instance, coping with stress, managing personal energy, and managing others. While we are not qualified psychologists, we have written these sections based on our practical experience of working with thousands of people, as well as accepting and working on our own personal and professional development challenges.

You will also notice that we don't ever talk about 'leading change'. This is because we believe this expression is a tautology. Leadership *is* change. Every single principle laid out in this book is about change, about adapting quickly to external changes and relentlessly improving internally to maximise value.

Finally, we toyed between going deep on a few topics or staying broad. After much debate, we decided on the latter as we wanted to offer an integrated, rational and emotional toolkit for leading a business and maximising value – we were focussed on offering the reader a set of tools that either individually or collectively would support better leadership. Of course, some topics may appear to be obvious, or the contents therein written as 'motherhood and apple pie' statements, but we wanted to offer a grounded, practical perspective where each element is connected into a superior approach to leadership. As such, we have so much more to offer on all the topics but had to keep the book to what, we hope, is a manageable size. If you would like us to go deeper into any of the 'issues', then do reach out – contact details are in the back of the book.

Our Credentials

We think it is only right that we offer our credentials as supporting evidence for what you will find inside this book. We'd like to emphasise that we don't subscribe to the 'superman' archetype, which is so common in business, and do not aim to impress or put ourselves on a pedestal. Indeed, invaluable experience comes as much from one's failures as from one's successes. As such, we offer our credentials as a way, we hope, of giving you confidence that we, as authors, have 'been there and done that'.

In short, we have had the privilege of working in many different corporate environments and cultures for a combined total of over seventy years. We have worked together for nearly twenty-five years.

We won't bore you with long CVs, which you can always check on LinkedIn if you're interested. Instead, we would like to give you a taste of our collective and individual experience, which we have used as the basis for the book.

In our careers, together or individually, we have worked in:

… public limited companies, private limited companies, government-owned companies, start-ups, and mature businesses…

… head office, front office, middle office, back office…

… banking, technology, government, management consulting, auditing, private equity, and medical innovation.

We have climbed the corporate ladder from office junior to CEO and CEO adviser. In addition, we have applied our experience in the important roles of investors, non-executive directors, and Chairpersons.

We have complemented our practical experience with academic investment in the form of an MBA and other relevant qualifications.

We have managed complex stakeholders such as regulators, parliamentary committees, government shareholders, the Troika (European Commission, European Central Bank, and International Monetary Fund), institutional investors, unions, and other important customers.

We have worked in both fast-growth and challenged businesses. In terms of the former, we have developed and executed strategies to deliver profitable growth; as for the latter, we have negotiated, signed, and brought a company in and out of a European Commission Restructuring Plan.

We have worked in public and private capital markets by raising equity and debt, deleveraging assets, and restructuring balance sheets.

We have developed, refined, and used the key constructs offered in this book (Governing Objective, Vision, Management Model, etc.) relentlessly over the last twenty-five years in at least six different companies.

We have recruited hundreds of people and sat in ten times as many interviews. We have built teams and have let people go.

We have served as mentors and coaches to many junior managers, and we have adopted the same mindset as part of the leadership toolkit in this book.

Most importantly, however, we have the humility and the objectivity to understand that our professional journeys have encompassed both success and failure. Needless to say, we recognise all the pitfalls this book is trying to warn you about, as we have identified them from personal mistakes. We have both medals and deep scars. In short, we think we have a depth and breadth of experience that will be of enormous value to students of leadership, and it is our privilege to share it with you.

Finally, when we say 'we', we include the many thousands of good people with whom we have had the privilege to work with. This book would not have been possible without you.

Book Structure

This book is organised into four broad sections:

1: Creating an Organisational Blueprint. Here we discuss the foundational building blocks that any company with aspirations for high performance must put in place. These include Governing Objective, Vision, and Management Model. Collectively, we call them the 'Organisational Blueprint'. The Organisational Blueprint is the backbone or fuselage of high-performance organisations. By necessity, it has a structure and rigidity to it. Around it, though, is an opportunity for both creativity and flexibility. For example, whilst the Blueprint works equally well in start-up, scale-up, transformation, or business-as-usual corporate scenarios, very different management styles and strategies are required for each.

2: Shaping the Organisation. Here we set out the key structures and processes required to give a company direction and momentum. The most important topics in this section are Organisational Structure and Resourcing, Organisational Culture, and Operating Rhythm.

3: Managing Oneself. Here we argue that one of the most important prerequisites of leading, motivating, and managing others is the ability to manage oneself. The key topics discussed in this section include setting the right personal priorities and managing personal time and energy effectively.

4: Managing Others. Finally, we focus on developing one's leadership toolkit for managing others. The key topics included here are finding the best people for your company, embedding high-performance teams, using Reward and Recognition in the most effective way, adapting your management style to the situation at hand, and addressing the most common interpersonal conflicts in a constructive and effective way.

****

You can read this book in one of two ways: either chronologically or by scanning the table of contents for a particular issue of interest.

Finally, a comment on how we think about the positioning of this book. There is a swathe of well-written literature on all aspects of business whether that be sales, marketing, risk, strategy et al. However, whilst all are relevant, we are clear that all enterprises need strong foundations for how they run on a day-to-day basis, how they make decisions, how they allocate resources, how they manage performance, how they create the right conditions for success and, ultimately, how they create value. We argue that, without an integrated framework sponsored by the CEO and understood throughout the organisation, the chances of 'winging it' increase exponentially. In this book, we offer such an integrated framework that we argue is a prerequisite for sustainable success.

We hope you find this book both practical and authentic.

SECTION 1: CREATING AN ORGANISATIONAL BLUEPRINT

There are certain building blocks that need to be put in place in any company to set the conditions for high performance. We call these blocks the Organisational Blueprint. This defines why a company exists and how it is to be led and managed. Everyone in the company must know what the Blueprint elements are and use them consciously to guide decisions.

The Blueprint is based on the two key sides of human nature: the rational and the emotional. Unless both are explicitly addressed, a company is unlikely to endure the test of time. Negative consequences of not having a Blueprint or getting the blocks wrong include:

- Lack of clear company priorities
- Disjointed and inconsistent decision-making
- Misallocation of resources
- Destruction of value
- Disconnected (confused) colleagues

Section 1 is organised as follows:

Key Tools

Chapter 1: Governing Objective addresses the single most important question in any company: 'Why are we in business in the first place?' The answer to this question should guide all decisions in the company, including strategy and allocation of resources.

Chapter 2: Compelling Vision addresses how to give tangible meaning to colleagues in achieving the Governing Objective. It addresses the emotional needs of people working in the company.

Chapter 3: Management Model addresses aligning the company's Value Goals, Risk Appetite, Strategy, Financial Targets, and Strategy Execution within a rational Management Model, thereby enabling the delivery of the Governing Objective.

Stumbling Blocks in Implementing the Blueprint

Chapter 4: Strategy vs. Execution discusses the risks of choosing to emphasise strategy over execution or vice versa. Many executives have a natural preference for one or the other, but this is a bias that they cannot afford.

Chapter 5: Avoiding Gaming reviews the practice of 'gaming' the planning process and how to put a stop to it once and for all.

Key Capabilities for Implementing the Blueprint

Chapter 6: Decision-Making discusses the principles behind effective decision-making, which must be aligned with the Governing Objective and be consistent across the whole company.

Chapter 7: Customer Value outlines the principles of how to focus on your customers without destroying value for your shareholders. It's an important skill that many company executives routinely misunderstand and mismanage.

Chapter 8: Effective Investor Relations discusses how to close the gap between the intrinsic and extrinsic valuation of the company by operating an effective Investor Relations function.

Chapter 9: Measuring Value Creation outlines the principles for measuring progress towards the Governing Objective and the metrics that are most suitable to do this.

1. The Governing Objective: What Is It for Your Company?

Issue: Unless everyone knows why the organisation is ultimately in business, it is impossible to prioritise resources and activities effectively.

It is a statement of fact that an organisation exists to create value for specific groups of people. What may be unclear for many inside and outside an organisation is the governing – or primary – group that an organisation ultimately serves, as accountability to many is accountability to none. Indeed, if the Governing Objective is not specifically defined and communicated throughout the organisation, it will bring unintended consequences.

Unsurprisingly, many CEOs, senior managers, and employees at any level of the corporate ladder are often confused as to whom they should be creating value for. Of course, there are many stakeholder groups who lay claim to the value created by companies and the resources needed to produce it. Unfortunately, business and academic circles differ as to which they consider the primary group: is it the owners, the customers, the employees, the management, society, the environment, someone else, or a combination?

We can already hear your objections: why try to maximise value for a specific group and not maximise the value for all groups, or at least create value for all of them, at the same time? This seems like a fair solution.

In theory, this should be easy to accomplish – create a value equation that maximises the value for all stakeholders' groups simultaneously, subject to a set of limited resources and other constraints such as the level of risk taken and the environmental impact. Indeed, some academics have argued that this is achievable using balanced scorecards. The practical challenge is that such an equation is extremely complex to create and solve.

As practitioners, we claim that balancing the interests of all groups is an impossible task, and the result is a giant compromise in which no single stakeholder group is happy with the outcome. Each group will always fight for more, and corporate management can easily turn into a game of conflict resolution. The balancing act itself is not only widely open to various interpretations and challenges but is also nearly impossible to communicate clearly to all stakeholders. Often, this situation has many possible solutions (in the form of trade-offs between stakeholder groups), but it is impossible to justify one specific trade-off.

For example, if we want to maximise value for owners, employees, and customers all at the same time, then these simple questions become virtually impossible to answer and communicate:

- Which projects to invest in and why?
- What products to sell or stop selling and why?
- Which customer segments to focus on and why?
- Which people to hire, keep, or let go and why?

The practical reality is that running a business inevitably requires a constant stream of trade-offs, and without a steady reference point, these trade-offs will always look like a random set of guesses as to whose interests we are trying to balance.

The main alternative to balancing the interests of all stakeholder groups simultaneously is picking a primary stakeholder group and maximising the value for that group alone, subject to a set of minimum requirements for the other groups. For example, a company's leadership can choose to maximise the value to its customers subject to a set minimum return to its owners (for example, the cost of equity) or set minimum value to its employees (for example, in the form of working conditions and remuneration). As we will demonstrate later, the problem with this approach is that choosing to maximise the value for any stakeholder group except the owners can lead to unfavourable side-effects for all stakeholder groups – including those who take the greatest level of financial risk.

For instance, a few years ago, we participated in a global banking conference, during which the CEO of a bank, which had publicly chosen to maximise the value for its customers, gave a proud talk on the topic. While the metrics showed impressive customer experience outcomes, at no stage did the CEO comment on financial returns. At the end of the talk, we asked about the returns the bank was generating for its owners. It was clear from the answer that relative returns to owners were not as impressive (and less than the required hurdle rate). This example highlights why maximising value for any stakeholder group other than the owners is an unsustainable strategy.

At this stage, we need to be crystal clear that a relentless focus on Owner Value must not ignore the need to create value for other stakeholder groups as a supporting means of delivering sustainable returns; but means and ends must never be confused – more on that later.

Principles

Having a Governing Objective or selecting a primary stakeholder group for which to maximise value allows us to solve the value optimisation equation in practical terms. Otherwise, there is no solution or, even worse, there are too many solutions that are impossible to choose from. From a practical point of view, choosing a Governing Objective for a company must be based on the following three principles. It must:

- Be consistent with the reason the company is in business in the first place
- Be straightforward to measure and communicate
- Be a convenient and practical trade-off tool

Let's look at a classical company set-up in which management, staff, customers, and owners represent the list of stakeholders which an organisation might chose as its primary group to serve. We will touch upon special cases in which some of these groups coincide later.

Alternative 1: Maximising Management Value

This essentially means that all value generated by the company is distributed to management as remuneration. Ex-management staff are given the minimum reward possible, and customers are charged the maximum that management can get away with. The return to the owners is the lowest possible in the industry.

Unless this company was created to enrich management in the first place, this alternative is inconsistent with the first principle (to be consistent with the reason the company is in business). Of course, the owners are unlikely to remain invested for too long as they would be motivated to cash in their shares and invest in companies that are managed differently and can provide a better return.

Alternative 2: Maximising Customer Value

At first glance, this alternative is very attractive as it does not need to contradict the first and second principles. Proclaiming the need to serve customers in a value-maximising way is very powerful and is easy to measure and communicate. The challenge is that if we provide 'maximum value to the customer' without charging a commensurate price (including for the cost of equity), the company will go out of business in the long term as the value attributable to staff, management, and owners is the minimum possible. Same as above, owners are unlikely to stay invested for too long, and without them and the capital that they provide, business will cease to exist over time.

Alternative 3: Maximising ESG Value

ESG is an all-encompassing acronym for Environmental, Social, and Governance factors. Environmental factors include areas such as climate change, resource depletion, waste, pollution, recycling, and deforestation. Social factors include health and safety, working conditions, diversity, human rights, and local communities. Finally, governance factors include ethical standards, Board diversity, political lobbying and donations, and tax strategy.

Recently, ESG has become a very important element of many companies' strategies globally. As a matter of fact, many institutional and individual investors require companies to have a pronounced ESG strategy. It is then a legitimate question of whether companies should be managed to maximise their ESG value.

We argue that if ESG value is maximised as a priority, then the owners of the company are unlikely to stay invested for too long, as the value attributable to them would be minimum, and they can likely get better returns from alternative investments. We believe that companies should focus on delivering sustainable returns and disagree with those who believe it is the role of private enterprise to participate in social or political agenda unless there is a clear line of sight to value creation (which, in our experience, is very difficult to prove). We argue that without the specific consent of the voting majority of shareholders to engage in a non-sustainable value-maximising agenda, then neither the Board nor management has the legitimacy to do so.

Of course, this does not mean the ESG is unimportant or that it should be neglected. All this means is that ESG factors should be regarded as input to, rather than an output of, Corporate Strategy.

Alternative 4: Maximising Owner Value

It is clear that the only remaining viable alternative is to manage a company to maximise the sustainable value for its owners. Only then will the owners remain invested. If their returns exceed the returns they can get elsewhere, then owners will continue providing capital for further growth and investment. Without going too deep into corporate finance theory, we would like to mention that the riskier or more volatile a business is, the bigger the return the owners will expect.

Managing for Owner Value fits very well with the three core principles. First, most businesses are started by their owners to create value for themselves. Second, measuring and communicating owners value as a Governing Objective is, indeed, straightforward. Third, it allows management to make conscious trade-offs.

Why Did Shareholder (Owner) Value Get Such a Bad Name in Recent Times?

Maximising value for shareholders gained a lot of popularity in the late 80s and 90s but since then has gained a bad name due to the wide-spread belief that this value comes at the expense of customers, employees or the environment.

Certainly, bad corporate behaviours have contributed to these views, but at their core, these beliefs are incorrect. In fact, mistreating customers or employees certainly does not maximise Owner Value as, in the long run, these critical stakeholder groups can always choose to leave, which will inevitably lead to the demise of any company. In cases where these groups cannot leave, such as in monopolies and/or large geographical employers, it is up to the industry regulators to fix issues if companies are unwilling to do so themselves. Even in such cases, long-term mistreatment of customers and/or employees is likely to lead to a bad ending for the company. The critical point is that maximising the value for owners of the company and creating value for all other stakeholder groups are not mutually exclusive.

An example of something giving rise to poor corporate behaviour was that some managers (and many commentators) confused value with profit. Value is a long-term measure that implies sustainability. Maximising shareholder value really means maximising long-term sustainable shareholder value. If you look at it this way, mistreating customers and employees or damaging the environment do not maximise Owner Value. On the contrary, it is equivalent to destroying value in the long term.

Profit, on the other hand, is short-term in nature and usually measured in the corporate accounts on a yearly basis. Maximising profit will invariably lead to customers, employees, or the environment footing the bill in the long run. This is not what having a Governing Objective to maximise sustainable Owner Value means. Of course, a company must plan to have their profit targets aligned to long-term value creation (see Chapter 3) and cannot have a portfolio of 'J-curve' initiatives – but value must always be the primary measure.

To ensure that sustainable shareholder value is generated, the Governing Objective must be linked to corporate governance. It is the explicit role of the Board to ensure that sustainable long-term value is delivered to the owners of the company but not at the expense of other key stakeholders. This is done through a set of what we call 'sustainability' tests. We will explain these tests in more depth in Chapter 3, but they fundamentally test the alignment of the long-term, value-maximising strategy against various resource constraints and short-term objectives, e.g., alignment with short-term profit and cost targets or alignment with fair customer outcomes. Sustainability Tests allow management to maximise the value to the company's owners without both falling into the trap of balanced scorecards and compromising long-term value for short-term profit.

Actions

You can look at shareholder value as being the fruit a tree bears over time. If we focus solely on the fruit, we will be powerless to impact sustainable outcomes. However, if we focus on the factors that feed the tree, such as sunlight, water, and soil quality, then the tree will bear fruit year after year.

So, what do we need to do to create sustainable value for owners? In our experience, it is critical to put processes and feedback loops in place that will facilitate value creation over the long term. In very broad terms, these processes should include:

1. Strategic Planning – the outcome of this process is the long-term strategy of the company, which aims to maximise sustainable value subject to Risk Appetite and a series of Sustainability Tests.

2. Financial Planning – the outcome of this process is twofold:
- A three-to-five year medium-term Financial Plan expressed as an income statement and balance sheet
- A short-term (first-year) plan, also called the 'Budget'
- Capital and Liquidity Plans
- Stress Tests

3. Management Agenda – the outcome of the planning process is to define the set of highest-value issues and opportunities which the company is facing, and which must be resolved for value to be created.

4. Performance Management – the outcome of this process is a set of individual objectives for every employee, which link to the Strategic Plan, Financial Plan and the Management Agenda, accompanied by a clear understanding of where each individual contributor has (or has not) delivered on the journey to creating sustainable value.

We will explore these processes in more depth in the later chapters of this book. At this stage, we would like to stress the following:
- Increasingly more investors are analysing companies through the lens of ESG. In response, we argue strongly that unless you have a

Governing Objective and a clear set of Sustainability Tests – including agreed ESG outcomes – it would be impossible to make the right decisions in these areas without impacting the company's long-term survival.

- Pursuing the Governing Objective must be underpinned by clear and honest communication. In this regard, internal communications are critical to ensure that employees at every level of the corporate hierarchy are equipped with the information and tools to make the correct trade-offs. External communication is also critical because unless you run your own company, investors are most often not privy to the inner workings of the company they own. To return to our previous fruit metaphor, external investors can only see the fruit the tree bears. Thus, it is very important to keep investors in the loop as to how management intends to produce value. For both internal and external communication, having a Governing Objective provides a foundation for tailoring messages that are consistent, logical, and unambiguous.

Potential Pitfalls

Sometimes, certain stakeholder groups can overlap. For example, when customers and owners overlap, it results in a Co-Operative. Or, when management and owners overlap, it becomes a Family Business. In these cases, maximising Customer Value for the Co-Operative or maximising value for the Family Business are sensible Governing Objectives. However, one should recognise that the primary objective is still to generate value for owners.

You must also recognise at the very beginning that most employees, including management, may not be intrinsically motivated by the Governing Objective of maximising sustainable shareholder value. Despite its intellectual and logical power, this Governing Objective is not something that inspires people. As a matter of fact, the Governing Objective is a terrible motivational tool in and of itself. This is why the CEO and the Board need another tool that translates the Governing Objective into something that captures the hearts and minds of everyone working for the company. We have dedicated the next chapter to this matter.

2. The Vision: How to Set a Compelling Vision for Your Company

Issue: A well-defined Governing Objective is not enough on its own to motivate the people working for the company on a daily basis.

Defining a Governing Objective in the form of 'maximising sustainable owners' value over time' is essential as it gives management the clarity to make consistent decisions and resource trade-offs. However, we have discovered that a well-defined Governing Objective on its own is not a good people-motivator. Even if there is a monetary reward for achieving the Governing Objective in the form of an annual performance bonus or long-term incentive plans, this alone is insufficient as most people are not solely motivated by money. It is well known that money is a 'hygiene' factor; that is to say, people will work very hard to earn it, but after a certain remuneration level, which allows for one's basic needs to be satisfied, it ceases being the main motivator for performance.

Let's face it, most people are driven much more by their emotions than by abstract ideas, such as a Governing Objective. If you ask the people in your company what they want to achieve in their lives, given that money is enough to cover their basic needs, the vast majority will say that they want to make a difference in the world, help others, or achieve something extraordinary. No one will say that they wake up in the morning with the desire to make more value for the owners of the company.

For the Board and Management, it is, therefore, imperative to address these emotional needs by setting up a Vision – a more personal and concrete objective – that people can associate themselves with while, at the same time, maintaining the primacy of the Governing Objective.

Principles

Rational And Emotional Sides of Management

In people management, one must distinguish clearly between the rational and emotional sides of running a company. Both elements must be present in the effective leader's toolkit.

The rational side is concerned with facts, strategy alternatives, and rational decisions based on those facts. It governs the key company processes and its Organisational Structure. We have called all the tools for the rational side the 'Management Model'. The Management Model configures the company to achieve its Governing Objective and is the subject of Chapter 3.

The emotional side is not at all concerned with facts, processes, and structures. Rather, it is guided by a Vision to ignite people's – from the Chairman of the Board to the most junior employee – intrinsic motivation to be a part of something bigger than themselves. That something could be making a difference in the world, helping people improve their lives, or achieving something extraordinary. Most people should feel their company's Vision as something close and personal or as something they associate deeply with. In other words, the Vision is what brings the Governing Objective to life.

Relying either on the rational or emotional side only limits the possibilities available to a company. Performance is only maximised by integrating both the rational and the emotional elements into achieving the company's Governing Objective.

Definition of Vision

The word 'Vision', much like the word 'Strategy', has been widely overused in management literature over the past four or five decades. It has been used in different contexts and with many different definitions. For clarity, we define Vision as the combination of the organisation's Purpose, Values, Behaviours, and Operating Manners – in partnership with a rational Management Model, these are the key enablers of delivering the Governing Objective. Let's look at each component in more detail.

Purpose

We define Purpose as the reason for being, or the 'raison d'être', of the company itself. We prefer the term 'Purpose' to 'Mission' because it carries more of an emotional connotation. Thus, 'Purpose' fits our definition better. The 'reason for being' of any company should be compelling enough to motivate anyone who works there to adopt that Purpose as their own. If they can't easily do that, then the Purpose needs to change.

Purpose can start with 'We exist to…' or with 'We are in business to…', or just with 'To…'. A good example is IKEA's Purpose: 'To offer a wide range of well-designed, functional home furnishing products at prices so low that as many people as possible will be able to afford them.' Notice how the Purpose informs and guides everyone working for the company as to why they are in business in the first place. Also notice that it is quite easy and inspiring for employees to adopt this Purpose as their own, thereby satisfying their need for making a difference, helping people, or achieving something extraordinary.

Now let's first look at a bad example of a company's Purpose. A few years ago, we worked for a company whose Purpose was 'To become the most admired company in the world' in their industry. On the face of it, this Purpose might appear inspiring, but it left a lot of gaps in our understanding, e.g., Admired by whom? Admired for what? And how would being admired make any difference in our colleagues' lives?

Values

The second part of a company's Vision is its Values. We define Values as ways of being or the inner qualities that are shared by everyone working for the company. It's important to notice that a company does not have Values per se, as it is not a person with its own consciousness and mind. Therefore, Values are always personal, but when they are widely shared, they can be described metaphorically as belonging to the company. Some companies call them Core Values.

When describing the shared Values of a company, we like to use phrases that begin with 'We are…' followed by an adjective. Note how one can substitute 'We are…' for 'I am…' to describe one's own deeply personal way of being.

Values are essential to a company's Vision because they guide everyone as to the bespoke ways of being required for the success and delivery of the Governing Objective. In addition, Values strengthen the sense of belonging to the group.

Behaviours

This brings us to the third element of the Vision, which is Behaviours. Behaviours are the professional standards a group should aspire to live by each day and to which they should hold each other accountable.

It is important to understand how Values guide Behaviours. We would like to explain this with a simple example. Say you would like to lose weight. Most people approach this by focusing on their behaviours, i.e., eating less and/or exercising more. Unfortunately, many ultimately fail to lose weight because the personal will which we apply to maintain these behaviours sooner or later runs out. Those who succeed seem to have accessed something much deeper because the desired behaviours seem to happen without any forceful application of will. We assert that the initial change, whether conscious or sub-conscious, must be to one's way of being or values concerning health. Values always come first, and Behaviours follow second.

Operating Manners

Some companies elect to go even further and specify the minimum required operating standards for day-to-day working. In the past, we have sometimes called these standards 'Operating Manners'.

Operating Manners can both help employees be more effective in their interactions and build psychological safety in the working environment. We recommend that Operating Manners be defined as actions, such as: 'We come prepared to meetings', 'We stick to timing', 'We clarify when something is unclear', or 'We turn off mobile phones'.

We have found Operating Manners to be very useful in setting the minimum standards for a high-performing workplace.

Codifying Values, Behaviours, and Operating Manners

There is a lot of confusion and misunderstanding with regard to Values, Behaviours, and Operating Manners in the corporate world. Many companies commit three critical errors.

First, they codify values that are neither distinctive nor specific to the company. For example, a famous company, which shall remain unnamed, lists some of its Values as Leadership, Integrity, and Passion. Other companies list Authenticity or even People Centricity as values. None of these are bad in themselves, and they do carry a lot of meaning, but aren't they a 'minimum standard'? We recommend that you spend time and resources on defining Values that are specific to the company and not the 'minimum standard'.

Second, they mistake Behaviours for Values. We call this error the 'big mishmash'. Instead of 'We are…' (Values), the Values are described as 'We do…' (Behaviours). On a sub-conscious level, this error confuses employees as they cannot easily identify with or align with Values when they are being told what to do.

For example, many companies will list a shared value as something such as 'We focus on our customers'. It then needs another sentence or two to explain what 'customer focus' means, making it difficult for employees to make good choices when guided by such a 'Value'. Notice how much more powerful it is to say, 'We understand and act on our customers' needs'. This (real) value immediately guides everyone to explore those needs and act on the back of their understanding without specifying what these actions should be.

Third, to attempt to solve the 'big mishmash' issue, some companies will formulate a 'Value' such as 'We are customer-focused' or just 'Customer Focus'. This runs into the final error, which is using abstract or difficult words or words whose definitions are widely open for interpretation. This will require each value to be accompanied by a definition and, very often, by an example of its application. This situation often leads to confusion for employees unable to make individual choices consistent with a specific value.

Co-Creation, Alignment, and Recognition

In our experience, the power of inviting the organisation both to participate in defining and, subsequently, embedding the Vision is enormous. The benefit of collaboration and accountability manifests itself in the highest level of discretionary energy.

In addition, we always set ourselves the test of ensuring that there is a clear line of sight between the Governing Objective, the Management Model, and the Vision; in simple terms, we need to satisfy ourselves that there is no inherent conflict between the components.

Lastly, we have found enormous power in recognising people's commitment to the Values and Behaviours through, for example, an annual Recognition Event, where colleagues recognise and nominate each other.

Actions

Setting a Vision cannot be done in isolation in the Boardroom or the office of the CEO. If the Vision is to last and be used as intended, it is necessary to involve broad segments of colleagues or their representatives in the drafting.

How you set the Vision depends on the size of your organisation. For start-ups, it could be done by the founders at the earliest possible stage in the company's life; thereby, everyone else is subsequently recruited into the founders' Vision, which is very powerful. Often, entrepreneurs live their own Vision, even if not necessarily codified formally, and everyone in the company gets to imitate them.

Smaller companies can follow an informal process; however, the job becomes more difficult as organisations grow bigger. It gets even more complicated if the big company already has some form of Purpose and Values, but they need changing for some reason, e.g., if their Values are mingled with Behaviours or their Purpose is not compelling enough.

In this case, we have found the following process useful:

1. At a joint meeting, the Board and the Executive Committee (ExCo) endorse the Governing Objective, which itself can be the subject of much ill-informed and misguided debate, so patience is key (see Chapter 1). Then, formulate the Purpose of the company. The session could be facilitated by an

external facilitator to guarantee a fair process and with a solution is not the lowest possible dominator (which can happen when dominant personalities hog the discussion).

2. The middle management of the organisation, i.e., everyone who reports directly to the ExCo, then tests, challenges and, ultimately, validates the Purpose. Then, the same group of people formulate the company Values, Behaviours, and Operating Manners. Both sessions are facilitated by selected members of the ExCo.

3. To complete the feedback loop, the Board and the ExCo check, challenge, and approve the complete Vision at a final joint session facilitated either by the Chairman or the CEO.

4. The Vision is then officially and ceremonially launched to all colleagues and possibly to investors.

There are three additional and important steps that should happen after this process is over:

1. Members of the ExCo and some of their direct reports could choose to codify (a limited number of) additional Values, Behaviours, and Operating Manners for their specific line of business or function.

2. The Values, Behaviours, and Operating Manners should be incorporated into the company's formal appraisal and reward process.

3. Finally, alignment with the Vision must be adopted as a sustainability test when debating strategic alternatives. We will expand on this later, but essentially this means that only strategies consistent with the Vision must be evaluated and ultimately pursued by the company.

Of course, there are other processes which could be used to set the Vision, and they should all be correct if the key principles above are being applied.

Potential Pitfalls

1. The words 'Mission', 'Vision', 'Purpose', 'Values', and 'Behaviours' have been used to various degrees and with different definitions by many companies in the last few decades. This can cause a lot of confusion around the Board and ExCo tables, especially if some of the participants have used

those terms in differing ways. The best way to overcome this pitfall is to spend enough time on definitions and the key principles in advance of formal agreement and subsequent adoption.

It's a mistake to assume that people's rational side is stronger than their emotional side. Thus, getting colleagues to align with the company's Vision is much more important than getting them to align with its Strategy. As a matter of fact, if they co-create the Vision, they are much more likely to align with the Strategy later.

2. Crafting the Vision in a very small inner circle can be tempting to many CEOs because they feel that they can control the process and the outcome more tightly. This, however, is a mistake that could be very costly in the long run. It is crucial to involve as broad a segment of colleagues as possible if the Vision is to be useful and not just a collection of nice sentences. It is the CEO's role to create the conditions for the best conversations, to debate the draft outcomes, to persuade and influence, and, ultimately, to coalesce colleagues around the right outcome to deliver the Governing Objective.

3. In large and distributed organisations, one should be careful not to suffocate the individuality of certain subsidiaries, large divisions, or important departments. This can easily happen if the Purpose and the Values of the corporate centre are imposed indiscriminately on all subsidiaries. Local businesses must be allowed to have local Visions that create unity and reinforce self-governance if it is in harmony with the Group Vision. Having a Local Vision that represents a local situation, environment, and time while respecting the Group Vision is the best outcome, as it fuses local involvement, ownership, and commitment with global belonging (the perfect match).

3. The Management Model: How to Design and Operate an Effective Management Model

Issue: To deliver the 'Governing Objective' requires both a Vision and a Management Model working in harmony.

So far, we have established that setting a Governing Objective is the fundamental foundation of a shareholder-led enterprise. In addition, we have noted that for the Governing Objective to have real meaning for stakeholders, it needs to be complemented by a compelling Vision. The final piece of the jigsaw is to define a rational Management Model.

Broadly speaking, the Management Model should be organised in a way to deliver five key elements: Value Goals, Risk Appetite, Strategy Development, Financial Plan and Strategy Execution. They, in turn, are supported and underpinned by a sixth element: the company's Organisational Structure. These elements flow logically from one to the other. Ultimately, all six must be inexorably connected, have a clear link to the Vision, and support the delivery of the Governing Objective – aka an integrated toolkit.

Below are some broad definitions:

1. The **Value Goals** are the rational and stretching but realistic and quantitative aspirations for the company. Value Goals are an input to strategy development and are not targets – targets are the outcome of the Strategic and Financial Plan that is to be performance managed.

2. The **Risk Appetite** is the explicitly defined level of risk that the company is prepared to accept in pursuit of its Governing Objective before action is required to reduce the risk.

3. The **Strategy** (or **Strategic Plan**) is an explicit articulation of the market and competitive choices made by the company at any point in time. That is, the company leadership must be clear about which markets they have chosen to participate in and how they have chosen to compete, e.g., by a unique customer offer, premium or discount pricing, or at a lower cost.

4. The **Financial Plan** represents the logical financial implications of the above strategic choices. It is an annual, multi-year model. The delivery of the Financial Plan and the associated KPIs become the delivery targets of the organisation.

5. The **Strategy Execution** (or **Execution Plan**) is the 'what/ how/ who/ why' of delivery. It includes all material commitments of Management to achieve the Financial Plan and deliver the Strategy (the highest-value issues and opportunities are defined in the Management Agenda).

6. The **Organisational Structure** is the organisational design of the company, including all the supporting people management processes such as Recruitment, Selection, Performance Management, Reward, and Recognition. Structure is the main vehicle through which accountability is distributed to executives, managers, and staff.

Unfortunately, in many companies, the key elements of Governing Objective, Vision, and Management Model are not as connected and integrated as they should be despite their leaders' best intentions. There are usually five types of disconnect that can be widely observed:

1. Disconnect between Purpose and Strategy. A disconnect between Purpose and Strategy will create a problem of leadership integrity for any company. It is usually the result of the Purpose being created in an ivory tower, without broad colleague participation or without subsequent embedding and alignment across the organisation. On the one hand, there is a Purpose that is supposed to create an emotional pull, and yet, on the other hand, the company's strategic choices do not align. For example, say the Purpose is: 'To improve the health and the lifespan of our customers', but at the same time,

the company is selling alcoholic beverages under a separate brand. Even if customers are not aware of this, the employees will know, and it will give rise to significant integrity issues.

2. Disconnect between Strategy and Organisational Structure. The Organisational Structure in most companies is the result of many years of tinkering to accommodate entries into new markets, M&A transactions, or even the personal aspirations of important executives. As a result, it is a patchwork of compromises, which in no way logically reflects the most up-to-date Strategy. This is an important issue to which we have dedicated Chapter 10 of this book.

3. Disconnect between Value Goals, Strategy and Financial Plan. This type of disconnect manifests itself in Strategy and Financial Plans that do not provide enough reasonable stretch towards the Value Goal. It is here that the process of debating facts and alternatives is so critical. The role of the Board is also important in checking and challenging that the management team are not 'lowballing' the plans. All things being equal, after each yearly iteration of the Strategy and the Financial Plan, the gap to closing the Value Goal should be getting smaller and smaller. See Chapter 5, where we discuss how to avoid 'gaming' the integrated strategic and financial planning process.

4. Disconnect between Strategy and Financial Plan. This type of disconnect is encountered way more often in the corporate world than it should be. It is usually the result of a lack of co-operation between the Strategy team and the Finance team, where neither has end-to-end responsibility for the planning process. The Vision and Strategy could be tightly integrated with one another, but the Financial Plan, which is supposed to follow logically from the Strategy, is modelled in isolation and follows a completely different process by, say, using an incremental percentage increase based off last year's numbers. This will always result in a deeply flawed inconsistency between the market and competitive choices made in the Strategy and the Financial Targets pursued by the company.

5. Disconnect between Financial Plan and Execution Plan. This type of disconnect is also very common and occurs when the Execution Plans are made in isolation from the Strategic and Financial Plans. A company can have

a consistent and integrated Vision, Strategy, and Financial Targets and still fail to accomplish any of them because the defined Execution Plans are inadequate.

While it is the role of the Board to test all corporate plans for consistency and the presence of the above disconnects, very rarely can this responsibility be found explicitly defined in the formal 'Matters Reserved for the Board'.

Principles

The company's CEO and leadership team must ensure end-to-end alignment between the company's Vision and Management Model (Value Goals, Risk Appetite, Strategy, Financial Plan, Execution Plan, and Organisational Structure) in delivering the Governing Objective. As detailed earlier, we call these three elements 'the Blueprint'. They are the foundation stones of every organisation. Therefore, the bigger the company, the bigger the alignment challenge.

Value Goals

In our experience, truly exceptional people and teams always aspire to get better and push the boundaries of performance. We have found that creating a culture of aspiration is a key leadership trait – it motivates, it inspires, and it stretches. We think that any leader who announces aspirational Value Goals and is credible and honest about the role of such Goals can create energy, ambition, and a delivery mindset across the organisation.

By setting Value Goals, the leader creates a shared ambition for the whole organisation. Value Goals also enable executives and Boards to focus their time on the highest-value strategic alternatives and to set reference points for Performance Targets by always seeking the business model and financial model that can close the gap to Goal in the best way.

There are a few but important principles at play when setting Value Goals:

1. Value Goals are different from Performance Targets. Even though Goals and Targets appear similar, they are very different in three crucial aspects:

- **Purpose:** Goals are broader and more general in nature and are used to set the general direction and ambition of the company.

Targets are more specific and concrete and are used to measure progress towards the Goals.

- **Timeframe:** Goals are always set over a longer term, while targets are typically short-term deliverables.
- **Strategy Development:** Value Goals reflect the company's aspiration and, as such, are an input to the strategy development process. Targets, on the other hand, are an output of the strategy development process and represent an internal or external commitment that must be achieved to deliver the company's strategy.

2. Value Goals must be sufficiently stretching without being demotivating. There is a fine psychological line one should never cross when setting organisational Value Goals. If you set Goals too low, they lose their aspirational nature, and people will be tempted to 'game' the system. If you set Goals too high, people will think that they are completely unachievable, and the Goals will become demotivating – exactly the opposite of their objective first place. Hence, to find the right balance between stretch and motivation, Goals must be set in the context of the company's Vision, and, if possible, relative to 'best' peer performance, however this is defined. In our experience, it is useful to benchmark the Value Goal against the performance of a competitor's peer set where, for example, top quartile Total Shareholder Return (TSR) over time can be used as a reference point for a stretching Value Goal.

3. Value Goals must be aligned with the key performance measures of the organisation. This principle establishes the clear link between Goals and Targets and, subsequently, the company's Governing Objective. In our experience, the best primary performance measures are TSR, Economic Value (EV), and Economic Profit (EP) (see Chapter 9 for more details).

4. Value Goals must be reviewed every year, but one should avoid a regular reset. While it is perfectly acceptable to change Performance Targets as often as external or internal circumstances change, changing Goals can create miscommunication and misunderstanding in the organisation. The company's Vision, combined with the associated Value Goals, is supposed to provide

long-term stability, direction, and aspiration for everyone working in the company.

5. Value Goals' setting process must not be overly complicated. While setting a Vision creates emotional alignment, setting Value Goals creates rational alignment. If people do not understand the process of Goal Setting, then creating rational alignment will certainly fail; as such, keeping it as simple (and explainable) as possible should be the approach.

Risk Appetite

Of course, risk is defined as the probability and impact/consequence of an event. In all businesses, there is the potential for events and consequences that constitute opportunities (upside) or threats (downside). Accordingly, a strong risk management and control environment is fundamental to protect and safeguard any company's performance and reputation. It follows that active risk management must form an integral part of the governance structure (Management Model) and is necessary for building trust amongst stakeholders.

In this regard, it is important to codify, and operate within, the boundaries of a Risk Appetite in order to avoid excessive risk taking, minimise potential losses and establish a robust risk culture as part of the company's overall ways of working.

We have always endorsed a risk management process of 5 key steps:

- Identification
- Assessment and Measurement
- Mitigation
- Monitoring and Testing
- Reporting and Escalation

A Risk Appetite Statement ('RAS') serves as a boundary to the business, enables a consistent approach to risk management, endorses risk discipline and integrates risk management into decision-making at all levels of a company. A well-structured RAS enables the company to maintain robust discussions of risk taking and management and provides a commonly understood baseline against which management recommendations and decisions can be debated, and effectively and credibly challenged (as a key part of Sustainability Tests).

The RAS should articulate how the company's appetite for, and tolerance of, risk will be expressed. This should come in the form of qualitative statements about the nature and type of risk that the company will take on, and quantitative limits and thresholds that define the range of acceptable risk. The RAS should include sub-statements for each distinct risk category and include actionable metrics and measures/indicators.

In our experience, it is a good practice to use 3 constructs when thinking about how to manage risk:

- Risk Capacity is the maximum level of risk a company can absorb given its current resources.
- Risk Appetite is the level of risk the company is willing to accept consistent with the Governing Objective.
- Risk Tolerance is a defined set of risk positions that require early intervention and correction to prevent a breach of a Risk Appetite threshold.

There a few but important principles at play when thinking about Risk Appetite:

1. The RAS must not constrain the strategy development process. It is important that the Board and Management Team have the freedom to debate the strategic and financial factbase, the insights therein and the alternative business models available for value creation. It may be that, for big strategic choices (participation and competitive choices), that Management presents a case to the Board to change the boundaries of the RAS; this must be the exception not the rule.

2. The RAS is a key element of the company's sustainability tests. The RAS, when articulated, must then be a key sustainability test for all Management Agenda items. It must be a (rare) conscious choice for the Board and Management to allocate resources for initiatives that fall outside the boundaries of the RAS.

3. The RAS is a key tool for managing risk at all levels of the organisation. We have found that the RAS is a critical element of the decision-making process. It provides the First Line of Defence (Management) with rules about the nature of acceptable risk taking, it gives the Second Line of Defence (Risk

Management) a clear reference point to opine on risk taking and the Third Line of Defence (Audit) a construct to provide independent assurance on the quality of risk management.

Strategy Development

There are a number of principles in this category that must be applied:

1. Strategy as a Set of Choices. There are many ways to consider strategy. Is it a grand vision of the future? Is it a process through which to get there? Is it discovering a completely new market that no one is yet contesting? Is it a sequence of moves in the market designed to deliver checkmate to competitors? Is it taking a specific competitive position? Is it adopting the best industry practices? Is it a set of key capabilities? Is it effective resource allocation? Is it creating a well-balanced Scorecard? Is it embracing flexibility in the face of ever-changing market forces?

We could continue for a while, and many strategy theoreticians have. While all these possible definitions and points of view on strategy have their own zealous proponents and specific practical application, many are inapplicable in practice and would fail companies more often than they would help them succeed.

In our view, the best practical definition of strategy is 'a set of choices'. We are not sure who the author of this definition is, but it most probably evolved out of Michael Porter's definition of competitive strategy: 'Competitive strategy is about being different. It means deliberately choosing a different set of activities to deliver a unique mix of value'.[1]

Generally speaking, there are two broad sets of choices that any company should make:[2]

- Which markets should we compete in?
- How do we compete in those markets?

The explicit answer to the first question defines the company's participation strategy. It can be further broken down into which product markets to play in,

---

[1] Michael Porter, Competitive Strategy: *Techniques for Analyzing Industries and Competitors*, The Free *Press*, Illustrated Edition, 1998.

[2] J. McTaggart, P. Kontes, and M. Mankins, *The Value Imperative: Managing for Superior Shareholder Returns*, The Free Press, 1994, Chapter 6, p. 86.

which geographical markets to be in, which customers to serve, and which distribution channels to occupy.

The explicit answer to the second question defines the company's competitive strategy. It can be further divided into (i) what unique benefits the company offers to its customers; (ii) how to set up the company's operations, including its supply chain, to deliver those benefits in the most efficient and effective manner; and finally (iii) to set a price position that maximises sustainable value to owners while delivering value to customers over and above the price paid for a good or service.

These two sets of choices, Participation and Competitive, together define a company's Strategy.

2. Making Effective Strategic Choices. Strategic choices represent the most important decisions that executives and Boards of directors must make over time and at any point in time. As such, following the principles of effective decision-making is crucial for developing and implementing a good strategy. These principles are expanded upon in Chapter 6. In this chapter we are going to outline their application in the context of making strategic choices.

• Facts

Before any decisions are even made, the company's executives must be clear on the facts that they are facing in the real world. In practical terms, decision-makers should always be looking for insights into where value is created or destroyed. A good strategic factbase covers everything pertinent to any Participation and Competitive choice to be made.

There is a simple rule that we have always followed: there must be enough facts behind every strategic question that needs addressing. As a minimum, the company should cover its product/service markets, geographies, distribution channels, customers, propositions, operations, pricing, and profitability. Each of these dimensions must also be evaluated from two perspectives: (i) the company's, e.g., how much economic profit the company is making in any given market, and (ii) the competitor's, e.g., how the company's economic profit stream compares to its competitors. Over the years, we have developed a very clear idea as to what a good strategic factbase looks like.

We are crystal clear that the development of a great factbase requires both quantitative and qualitative capability; we think that a great Strategy team should have a mix of data scientists/analysts (who are comfortable with detailed financial analysis) and strategy development managers (who are comfortable interrogating data to create insight and choices for management to debate).

- Alternatives

Every strategic choice must be considered against its alternatives. Otherwise, it won't be possible to tell whether this choice is value-maximising.

Many companies look at each of the Participation and Competitive strategy choices and consider them in isolation. This is a recipe for disaster because this method usually misses the big picture. Instead, what good companies do is look at the various strategic alternatives, where each alternative is made up of an integrated set of choices along both the Participation and the Competitive dimensions. The key tests are distinctiveness and coherence.

- Clear Decision Rules

Having clear Decision Rules is the third important element of effective strategic choice. Essentially, this means having explicit criteria to evaluate the strategic alternatives.

Based on what we have written in previous chapters, perhaps you will be unsurprised to learn that the number one Decision Rule is the Governing Objective – that is, the preferred strategic alternative is the one that maximises owner value over the long term.

Unfortunately, it is not always that simple, as there are several other conditions that must be considered. For example, is the preferred alternative aligned with the Purpose and the Values of the company? Does the preferred alternative also generate value for other stakeholders (e.g., customers or ESG stakeholders) while maximising value for owners? Does the preferred alternative fall within the company's Risk Profile or Risk Appetite (as the banking term goes)? What is the preferred alternative's financial profile over time? Management should pick the alternative that maximises value subject to a set of explicit constraints, which we call Sustainability Tests. In Chapter 6, we explore the subject of decision-making in greater detail.

Finally, if a certain course of action seems obvious due to the pragmatic experience of the decision-maker, it must be tested quickly but rigorously. However, the default position must be that if it is a big strategic decision, even if the answer might sometimes appear obvious, using the decision-making standards detailed above is always justified.

Financial Plan

The key principle underpinning the creation of a Financial Plan is implementing a single planning process, which integrates strategy, financial forecasting, and operational planning. Many companies operate three different processes, often owned by three different executives, which are supposed to integrate but never really do. Having a single process is thus critical.

A good Financial Plan should also enable the dynamic calculation of the company's intrinsic value, i.e., the value of the company calculated based on insider information underpinned by the Strategic Plan. It is not the market value of the company as represented by its share price but a much more accurate estimation. In the long run, the market value should always track the intrinsic value. The intrinsic value per share provides the key guiding light for how the Investor Relations team speaks to the market in terms of guidance.

Strategy Execution

The key principle here is linking Reward to Performance. This reinforces personal accountability and attaches tangible consequences to decisions. Every person working in the company should have specific objectives linked to the Governing Objective, the Vision, and the Management Model, all of which should be evaluated periodically. Managing performance is the topic of Chapter 22.

An Example

We know of large businesses and specific executives that did not believe in formal strategy. They saw it as limiting. They thought they themselves knew all the facts. They thought that no one could surprise them with anything new.

They considered spending money on developing a factbase and strategy alternatives a waste of time.

As a result, there was a big gap between the de-facto strategy, the financial forecasts, and the day-to-day Strategy Execution. There were too many pet projects, a fundamental misallocation of financial, human, and IT resources, and (despite protestations to the contrary) a real lack of engagement with colleagues – which, ironically, was the missed opportunity. Perhaps most importantly, there was a lack of integrity (defined as without fact-based evidence) as to what the most important issues and opportunities to be focused on were, with a distinct lack of courage to say 'no'. This is a good example of extreme pragmatism killing new ideas and positive challenges. 'Thinking' takes backstage to 'doing'.

Of course, many other companies often fall prey to the opposite problem: too much thinking and very slow movement toward their desired direction. Both approaches are equally wasteful; hence, our passion for a connected Vision and Management Model.

Actions

Align the Elements of the Blueprint

The critical success factors in achieving alignment are:

1. Vesting the responsibility for implementing and managing the single integrated planning process to a dedicated Strategy and Planning Team. Many companies hand over the key planning responsibilities to their Finance teams; however, in our experience, this is always a sub-optimum solution as finance professionals tend to apply their own biases (for example, near-term profitability at the expense of long-term value or 'cost out' without differentiating between 'good cost' and 'bad cost') and often tend to ignore the broader strategic context in which the company operates.

2. Introducing a common language and terminology across the organisation, which supports the alignment of interests. It is obvious that common language and terminology allow people to understand each other better, and yet this is ignored in many companies. Depending on who you ask, terms such as Vision, Mission, Strategy, and Management Model have different

definitions. Unless management takes the time to codify and apply common terminology, there will always be misunderstandings in the Boardroom. In addition, value-based metrics, such as EP and EV (see Chapter 9 and Glossary of Terms), should also become common terms in any value-based organisation. The vocabulary at the end of this book is a good starting point for the kind of language that we have found useful over the years.

3. Working off the same set of facts. Many companies do not bother to unify the set of facts that they are using. This means that the Strategy team and the Finance team might work off a different set of assumptions, say, about the size and growth of a particular market. A common (and detailed) factbase, which covers detailed product/channel/customer economics as well as the markets and the competitive dynamics, is a must.

4. Implementing an Organisational Structure that delegates responsibility and accountability in a way that supports the company's Strategy. In management science, there is the perennial debate about what comes first: Strategy or Structure. In our experience, Structure is always a support factor for Strategy, and it must be treated as such. See Chapter 10 on Organisational Structure for further information.

Set Value Goals

1. Set Value Goals along three performance dimensions (TSR, EV, and EP), if possible. A key principle that we pointed out earlier in this chapter is the requirement for a clear link between Goals and key performance measures. As we detailed in Chapter 9, we have a clear view that the Board, the CEO, and the ExCo of any shareholder-owned business should have three primary – and mandatory – performance measures (which could then be supplemented by other strategy or market-linked KPIs):

- TSR – to measure external value creation performance
- EP – to measure internal value creation performance over a single reporting period
- EV – to measure internal value creation performance over multiple reporting periods

Bringing this logic into Goal Setting, a company should set, at minimum, performance aspirations along the above three lines (or as close a proxy as possible).

2. Approach Goal Setting in two ways: (i) an integrated bottom-up approach, or (ii) a simple top-down approach. For example, we worked for a mature organisation that had an integrated approach and used a factbase of peer performance to calculate the top quartile TSR required for doubling the external value of the company over a fixed time period, which, in itself, required an annual stream of EP. The result was a set of Value Goals derived very rationally from the bottom up:

- Group TSR Goal – Top quartile performance relative to a competitor peer group
- Group EV Goal – Double Internal Value of the company every four years
- Group EP Goal – Defined EP Goals for every year of the four-year period

While advocating TSR, EV, and EP Goals, one also needs to be pragmatic based on the company's industry and maturity, in which case the second approach to Goal Setting might be more appropriate. For example, we worked with a start-up company that was trying to create a brand-new market, so a bottom-up peer benchmarking exercise was not possible. Therefore, the company's leaders set a simple top-down Goal of aspiring for €100m of annual recurring revenue in the next five years based on the belief of the Board that such a rational Goal would galvanise the organisation and lead to value maximisation.

3. Test Stretch and Ambition versus the Value Goal. The benefit of setting a Value Goal is that it gives Management and the Board a quantitative 'north star' to stretch strategic thinking – and the development of alternatives. In addition, it facilitates a rational debate about the level of ambition in the Financial Plan and the quality of the issues and opportunities codified in the Management Agenda.

Develop Risk Appetite

1. Establish an enterprise-wide Risk Appetite. The company should describe the aggregate level and types of risk that it is willing to accept, consistent with applicable law and the interests of all its stakeholders whilst respecting the primacy of the shareholder.

2. Use Risk Appetite to promote and embed a sound risk culture. A sound risk culture in any company drives and supports value creation over time by encouraging risk awareness, desired behaviours and sound judgement about risk taking.

3. Some other key actions might include:

- Sponsoring the RAS visually and vocally by the Board and Management
- Developing a clear and well-communicated RAS
- Executing superior decision-making with the RAS as a key Sustainability Test
- Taking personal accountability for controls and attestations
- Escalating threats and concerns rapidly, and implementing remedial actions in a timely manner
- Using failures as an opportunity to learn
- Encouraging openness and transparency in supporting all colleagues 'to do the right thing'

In summary, creating a working environment where it is safe and acceptable, without any blame, for all to raise any concerns about risk practices, processes or behaviours that do not meet the company's Vision.

Embed Strategic and Financial Planning

1. Introduce an annual Integrated Planning Process (IPP). All companies have planning processes, but not many integrate planning activities effectively. One way to ensure that planning is integrated is to give the end-to-end responsibility for the planning process to a single team or senior executive (in our experience, this should be the Strategy team).

2. Invest in Strategy and Planning expertise. The best place to vest the end-to-end responsibility for the IPP is the Strategy and Planning (S&P) Team.

In our experience, there is no consistency across companies as to whether they have S&P teams and how much investment is allocated. In our view, having a strong S&P team goes a long way towards removing the disconnects that we describe above.

3. Create and refresh a shared factbase. Knowing where value is created and destroyed is the starting point for many of the most important decisions in any company. It is equally important for all decision-makers to work off the same set of facts to ensure there are no disconnects. This is another area where investing in S&P expertise is greatly rewarding in the long run. In larger companies, we would recommend having both a central Strategy team who develops the 'Group' top-down factbase and set strategy development / execution standards and Business Strategy teams that deliver bottom-up strategy to group standards. This then helps the Board and CEO make resource allocation choices between Group and Business Unit initiatives.

A combination of deep quantitative expertise complemented by strong strategic thinking is the ultimate combination – or 'combine poets and mathematicians', as we say. In our experience, the best factbase is kept up to date in real time as new facts emerge. For example, as competitors introduce new products or pricing, it is critical that the company can pivot, react, or lead as new insight is gained. In addition, we would recommend that a full refresh of the factbase is undertaken annually as part of the IPP.

4. Formulate, Evaluate, and Debate strategic alternatives as part of the IPP. All critical strategic choices – from which markets to participate in to how to compete in those markets – should be evaluated and debated at least annually as new facts are added to the factbase. This is one of the most important steps in the IPP and the whole corporate calendar. In our opinion debating alternatives is one of the key attributes of a healthy culture – the absence thereof is usually a sign of a top team underpinned by hubris and arrogance (and which is underperforming).

Optimise Strategy Execution

1. Formulate a Management Agenda and update it regularly. Over the years, we have found that a Management Agenda tool is extremely useful for

ensuring alignment and prioritising resources.[3] It spans both Strategy and Execution, bringing them together in a way that helps management focus both their attention and time on what is most important at any given point.

In simple terms, the Management Agenda is the set of highest-value issues and opportunities facing the company. It has two main parts: the Strategy Agenda and the Execution Agenda.

The Strategy Agenda includes the set of highest-value issues and opportunities pertaining to the Strategy arising from the factbase/insights that have not been grounded and whose commitments are not in the Financial Plan. We like to think about the Strategy Agenda as the Research and Development Agenda for where future value can be created or destroyed.

The Execution Agenda includes the set of highest-value initiatives and/or projects pertaining to the existing Strategy/Business Model of the company. In other words, it includes the most important elements of the Financial Forecast.

The Management Agenda is a highly effective prioritisation tool which forces everyone in the company to focus on the right things. CEOs can also use the Management Agenda to shape the dialogues at ExCo and Board meetings, support 1:1 meetings with direct reports (see Chapter 14), track progress, and shape investor dialogues.

2. Link individual performance to reward. In accordance with the principles outlined above, there must be an explicit link between individual performance and reward. This does not necessarily mean that reward is purely expressed in financial terms. Timely recognition, career opportunities, mentorship, etc., could be seen as other forms of Total Reward which satisfy certain inherent human needs. We describe this in more detail in Chapter 23.

3. Build a compelling value narrative. Having a compelling and consistent story about where value is created (or destroyed) by the company is very important both internally for colleagues and externally for investors. The colleague narrative should motivate, inspire, and provide clear guidance on what's important (and what isn't). Understanding whether the intrinsic value

---

[3] 'Management Agenda' is term that we have borrowed from Marakon Associates.

per share is below, equal to, or greater than the market value per share at any point in time will shape the Investor Relations narrative. The CEO, the CFO, and every member of the ExCo must be well-versed in understanding the basic tenets of corporate finance (and valuation) and, consequently, the Value Narrative.

In our experience, a leadership team that cannot differentiate between external measures of performance (e.g., RoE; EPS; P/E ratio) and internal measures of performance (EP and EV) will find it very difficult to make the right strategic and financial choices in terms of resource allocation – at its simplest, how can a Board be assured that the CEO is maximising the long-term sustainable value of the business at any point in time if there are no measures associated with that governing responsibility? In summary, maximise the intrinsic value of the business (through the processes, tools, and measures described in this book), and market value will surely follow.

Potential Pitfalls

There are a number of pitfalls must be carefully avoided:

1. Beware of using the same approach irrespective of company size or maturity. The approach that we are recommending above is (generally) more suitable for larger companies that operate in more established industries. However, smaller companies can still follow a similar process (Facts, Alternatives, Decision Rules, Management Agenda, etc.) without many of the formalities. Moreover, if the company cannot afford an independent S&P Team, then the overall responsibility for the process can be taken over by the CEO or the CFO. Companies that operate in new or extremely dynamic industries face another problem; that is, their plans could already be obsolete by the time they are put down on paper. Planning could be extremely difficult in such situations. However, this does not preclude knowing the facts and evaluating the alternatives. It's just that the leaders of such companies must use their intuition, or 'executive intuition' as we would like to call it, in much higher dosages. There is more on this topic in Chapter 6 on Decision-Making.

2. Beware of creating a cumbersome and heavily bureaucratic planning process, which can stifle everyone involved. 'Thorough' does not need to be 'cumbersome'.

3. Beware of financial incrementalism, e.g., adding or subtracting 'X' per cent each year from the financial projections. This approach is tempting because it is so easy, but it rarely has anything to do with market and competitive reality.

4. Beware of allowing the Financial Plans to dictate the Strategy. This is destructive in the long run. It should always be the other way around. That is why vesting the responsibility of the IPP to the CFO or Finance Team can be risky if their strategic thinking lacks breadth.

5. Beware of the 'Yes' men who can sabotage even the most robust planning process. Such people agree with everything put on the table without responsible check and challenge. In all cases, we recommend that all senior executives justify their Strategic, Financial, and Execution Plans to the CEO, CFO, Chief Transformation Officer (CTO), and Chief Strategy Officer (CSO) – who play a contrarian role – every year during the IPP.

6. Beware of a lack of independent performance-tracking mechanisms. Our experience suggests the appointment of a senior CTO who holds ExCo to account for every line-item commitment in the Strategy, the Financial, and the Execution Plans – both business-as-usual and Management Agenda – is a critical and valuable hire.

7. Beware of executives gaming the process by arguing that everything in their realm of responsibility must be on the Management Agenda. This way, pet projects receive funding or resource allocation (e.g., IT support) that they otherwise would not have. The CEO, CFO, CTO, and CSO must be ruthless in the construction of the Management Agenda using 'directional value-at-stake' as the sole entry metric. This will ensure the Management Agenda has the highest-value issues and opportunities defined and funded. In our experience, planning any more than four to seven items on the Agenda is a recipe for sub-optimal performance. Management must be ruthless and disciplined in the allocation of resources, even if it means saying 'no' or upsetting some of their colleagues.

8. Beware of senior executives claiming to be strategy experts and trying to intervene in the work of the S&P Team. Not everyone with an MBA can be a strategist. The key is for the CSO to act as the 'Second Line of Defence' by setting the standard, so all strategy is developed to the same quality, within reason, using common templates (this is where the power of PowerPoint and Excel come into their own), applying the same language and measures, and subjecting each ExCo member (Business Units and Functions) to check and challenge before submission to the CEO (who has a right of veto).

4. Strategy or Execution: Which Is More Important?

*Issue: **Top leadership cannot afford** any **bias in terms of time or resource allocation when developing and executing the Strategy, as this is bound to create a fatal disconnect between the two.***

There has been a decades-long debate in management literature about which is more important – the company's Strategy or its Execution. The two schools of thought can be summarised as follows.

Some believe that Execution is more important because, without proper Execution, even the best Strategy will fail. Therefore, Strategy is completely dependent on Execution, and hence it is where the CEO's and the Board's bias should be. This bias towards Execution is very well demonstrated in the following quote by Jack Welch, the legendary CEO of GE: *'In real life, strategy is actually very straightforward. You pick a general direction and implement like hell.'*

On the other hand, others believe Strategy is more important because it represents the company's set of choices regarding where to compete and how to compete. Therefore, Execution is completely dependent on this set of choices, and hence it is where the CEO's and the Board's bias should be. This bias towards Strategy is strongly implied in the following quote by Michael Porter, the father of strategic management: *'The essence of strategy is choosing what not to do.'*

What both schools of thought fail to recognise is that results are much more important than both Strategy and Execution. Let's be crystal clear; results are mutually dependent on both 'excellent thinking' and 'excellent doing'. In other words, both Strategy and Execution are two sides of the same coin called 'results'. All companies need both good thinking and good doing. They are not mutually exclusive; they are mutually reinforcing. They support and balance each other. To quote Sun Tzu from *The Art of War*: *'Strategy without tactics is the slowest route to victory. Tactics without strategy is the noise before defeat.'*

If, for some reason, the leaders of the organisation give priority to one or the other, then they will inevitably create a disconnect between Strategy and Execution, leading to all sorts of potential problems, such as:

- Executing too slowly or too hastily
- Looking for perfection
- Being confused by unclear priorities
- Pursuing pet projects that don't create value
- Misallocating resources in terms of time, people, and money
- Being unpleasantly surprised at the last minute
- Creating a culture clash between 'thinkers' and 'doers'

In our experience, the argument that Execution is more important is by far the most popular amongst senior leaders. This is not coincidental because most senior leaders start off at lower- and mid-level manager positions and are generally paid to execute strategic decisions, not make them. As they move up the corporate ladder, they naturally have a bias for 'doing'. In contrast, we will go so far as to say that 'good thinking' is one of the most inimitable sources of competitive advantage. Perhaps the abundance of consultants demonstrates a market niche for 'thinking' that reflects poorly on companies' ability to develop the internal capability of strategic management. In our experience, third-party advice is an invaluable tool in a company's toolbox; however, there is a clear distinction between the legitimate use of consultants to help manage a crisis or create execution momentum versus filling a capability gap that really should be part of a company's DNA, e.g., through a Strategy and Planning Team.

Principles

'Thinking' and 'doing' are both indispensable to 'results'. In the corporate context, 'thinking' is the Strategy, 'doing' is the Execution, and the 'results' are the delivery of the company's Governing Objective and Vision.

Having an excellent Strategy allows company leaders to face the uncertain future with confidence and without fear. Excellent Execution gives leaders the confidence they can handle anything that comes their way and pivot successfully if the Strategy needs repointing. Excellent results provide the raw material for investment, profitable growth, and shareholder return.

Good 'thinking' involves a measure of both facts and intuition, which must always be in balance. If decision-makers rely too much on intuition, the results could be random – good or bad. If, on the other hand, they over-rely on facts, the results could omit the value of 'good experience' (experience defined as twenty years of experience, not one year of experience twenty times). There is more information about this in Chapter 6 on Decision-Making.

Let's take as an example a particular financial institution which we reviewed a few years ago. Before the financial crisis in 2008, it was growing faster than everyone else in the market. It was smaller than its main competitors, and it was a price-taker in all its product markets. As a result of this, not a lot of thinking had gone into the Strategy, as management thought it was a waste of time. They were simply doing exactly what the bigger players were doing. One could say that their Strategy was 'imitation'. In addition, they believed that being world-class in Execution was the 'secret sauce'. It had worked thus far, and they were happy with the results – what could possibly go wrong?

When the global credit crunch struck in 2008, they were ill-prepared and surprised. Neither did they know where they created or destroyed value, nor did they have any distinctive competitive advantage that could have helped them soften the blow. Because they had done no deep thinking at all and were only gliding along with the competition, the results deteriorated badly and quickly.

Actions

There are a number of actions that could be considered:

1. Integrate Strategy and Execution into a seamless whole, leadership should create an explicit link between (i) the IPP and (ii) the Management Agenda. We discussed Integrated Planning in Chapter 3. The important point

we would like to reiterate here is that the responsibility for the complete end-to-end planning process should be given to one senior leader and their team (typically the S&P team), thus reducing the risk of disconnect in its constituent parts.

The way integration of Strategy and Execution happens in the Management Agenda is also very important. Remember that the Management Agenda was the set of highest-value issues and opportunities facing the company. It has two main parts: the Strategy Agenda and the Execution Agenda. The tight integration between the two parts of the Agenda occurs as initiatives can only move from the Strategy Agenda to the Execution Agenda with Board-approved financial and operating commitments attached.

2. Create a balance between both high-quality 'thinking' and 'doing', the CEO and the Board must emphasise the prominence of both a strong S&P Team headed by a CSO and Transformation Team headed by a CTO. The CSO should have intellectual rigour, pragmatism, and resilience – in terms of the latter, be under no illusion that there will be some members of ExCo who either 'know best' or 'reject the process' (either overtly or covertly) or do not believe in the Governing Objective. The CSO must have real 'bite', backbone, and assertiveness, knowing that they have the full support of the CEO.

The CTO should have a relentless focus on holding Business Unit and Functional leaders to account for promises in the IPP. The CTO should be detail-focused, relentless in the pursuit of delivery, systematic in their approach, and ready to raise 'off-track' performance to the CEO when early signs of 'drift' begin to appear.

Potential Pitfalls

Beware of the wrong attitude towards both Strategy and Execution. Some executives will attempt to game the process by ensuring their pet projects land on the Management Agenda to claim resources. In this case, this must be counter-balanced by an independent Strategy Function that upholds the strategy development standards (that is, the standards of good thinking) of the company and the importance of linking initiatives to the Governing Objective and Vision. We have dedicated the following Chapter 5 to the process of spotting and avoiding gaming.

5. 'Gaming' The Planning Process: How to Avoid It

Issue: The practice of 'gaming' the strategic and financial planning process is a serious challenge for many companies around the world.

Gaming the system is typically a feature in companies whereby the planning process is not integrated and has many disconnects between its parts. What usually happens is that during the planning process, the CEO and CFO allocate targets to budget owners that significantly over-estimate the revenue targets and significantly under-estimate the cost and investment targets. Such top-down estimates are usually calculated by incrementalism, i.e., last year's number plus 'x' per cent. Managers, who are accountable for delivering these targets, naturally object and propose what they, in turn, think is achievable; that is, they significantly under-estimate the revenue targets and significantly over-estimate the cost and investment targets. What ensues is a messy negotiation process, where those who shout the loudest or have the most influence over their boss end up with more resources and fewer stretching commitments.

Often, this process is exacerbated by the tension between short-term results and long-term investment. We would argue that in many companies 'gaming' is considered a key part of the planning process, and managers at all levels of the company prepare in advance for the messy negotiations, pulling every available lever of influence.

'Gaming' is a serious issue because it:

- Fails to allocate resources to the highest-value issues and opportunities.

- Fails to produce targets that are both stretching and grounded in economic reality.
- Creates tension between the corporate 'Centre' and the portfolio 'Businesses'.
- Creates serious demotivation throughout the organisation.
- Wastes valuable management time.

Principles

There are a number of principles that must be applied:

1. We must start by distinguishing again between long-term Value Goals and short-term Targets. The long-term Value Goals must be stretching but realistic in nature and directly linked to the Governing Objective. The top-line Value Goal could sound something like 'We will double the value of the company to its owners over the next four years'. These Value Goals do not need to be 100% grounded in facts (although one should try), and it is acceptable not to know exactly how they are going to be achieved. It's enough to know that the Strategy Agenda will contain several identified high-value issues and/or opportunities during the planning cycle, which will close the 'gap to the Value Goal' if they prove doable after the appropriate strategic research (it is best practice to convert a Value Goal into an aspirational profit shape).

The short-term Targets are simply a combination of next year's budget and planning horizon Targets. These must be 100 per cent grounded in the existing economic reality. A well-researched factbase of product, customer, channel economics, and market and competitive dynamics must dictate what everyone in the company commits to. The short-term targets are defined in what we call the Financial Medium-Term Plan (MTP). It spans four or five years of financial projections and is by nature a mixture of grounded forecasts and aspirations. The Value Goal trajectory will be more ambitious than the MTP and must be aspired for on a rolling basis – once the MTP and Value Goal are aligned, it's time to reset the Value Goal.

2. There must be a healthy tension between short-term Targets and long-term Value Goals. This way, those accountable for the delivery of the commitments will sign up for both concrete short-term targets and long-term

aspirational Value Goals without being bullied into something they don't believe in. This will remove the tension between the 'unreasonable boss' and 'direct report gamers' inherent in the 'gaming' process; it will enable the focus of time and energy on how both to deliver commitments and bridge the gap between the short and long term. Naturally, therefore, the conversation about the short-term Targets focuses on the facts which do or do not support those commitments, and the conversation about the long-term Value Goals focuses on the strategic choices that must be made to create value in the longer term. Personalities, political influence, and connections across the company that are so important for 'gaming' lose their currency during such conversations.

Actions

There are a number of actions that could be considered:

1. Ensure that sufficient time and effort go into developing (and refreshing) the company's quantitative and qualitative factbase in advance of the planning process. It's important that a granular analysis of where value is created and destroyed in the company (across product, channel, and customer domains) is complemented by a broad perspective of industry and competitor trends. Factbase and Value Goal Setting are owned by Strategy, whereas the multi-year financial forecast models and Target Setting is owned by Finance in dialogue with Strategic Business Units (SBU) and Functions.

2. Create a business partnership model in which each SBU is supported both by a Strategy and a Finance Business Partner. Business Partners should help the businesses by standing in their shoes and simultaneously upholding the standards required by S&P and Finance, respectively. Thus, one group of people focuses on the now (Targets), and another group of people thinks of tomorrow (Value Goals) within the same SBU.

3. Discuss Value Goals and Targets for each SBU at a dialogue session with the CEO, where the focus is not on haggling up or down but on the facts, the expected competitive moves, the expected improvement of the SBU's competitive position, and the key issues/opportunities associated with the requested investments. It is up to each SBU and Function to use the facts to

demonstrate that their preferred strategy will deliver competitive advantage and value creation.

4. Allocate resources to all businesses and projects expected to produce positive value for their owners (allowing for execution constraints). If capital is not enough to fund all opportunities, raise capital from the market – the mindset must always be that 'capital is plentiful but expensive' and not 'capital is constrained but free'.

5. Link the Yearly Bonus to hitting the Targets and the Long-Term Incentive Plan (LTIP) to deliver the Value Goals.

Potential Pitfalls

Because 'gaming' is so popular in many companies around the world, many managers have learnt to expect it and have become very good at it. Even when a fact-based IPP is implemented in your organisation, some managers won't like dealing with facts and strategy and will try and 'game' the process anyway. They will often call themselves 'pragmatists' and try to depict the collection of the factbase as a waste of time or effort. Because they won't be able to easily 'game' their Targets, they will attempt to 'game' the Management Agenda. The solution to this problem is to be ruthless in the application of the above principles.

Others will publicly pretend to respect the fact-based approach to Value Goals and Target Setting, only to try and influence their bosses in off-the-record meetings. The CEO and CFO should not engage in such discussions and only discuss Value Goals and Targets at formal dialogue meetings as part of the IPP. In addition, the dialogue meetings should also be attended by the standard keepers (Strategy and Finance Business Partners), who must have checked and challenged all work before submission to the CEO and CFO to ensure the fairness of the process.

6. Decision-Making: How to Ensure It Is Effective

Issue: The decision-making process in many companies is not as effective as it could be, leading to a waste of resources.

Corporate leaders are paid to make decisions – and be accountable to the Board and Owners for the consequences. Essentially, this is the most important thing that they do. Yet, so many leaders make the most important decisions for their companies for completely the wrong reasons. Some examples include:

- Decisions based on fear. Say there is a new technology on the horizon that could potentially be a threat. Many consultants make a lot of money by skilfully scaring top executives about such potential threats.
- Decisions based on a desire to please everyone. The decision-maker wants neither confrontation nor disagreement, so decisions are based on consensus, which is the lowest possible denominator, and more often than not leads to a sub-optimal outcome.
- Decisions based on a desire for domination. Decision-makers with narcissistic tendencies often take on a particular decision trajectory because they want to maximise their own power and influence at the expense of either the organisation they work for or their colleagues (the so-called 'agency' problem).
- Decisions based on imitation. Such decision-makers' logic is: 'We're doing it because of the competition, and we can't afford to miss out.'
- Decisions based on over-eager competitive impulses. The logic here is: 'We're doing everything possible to beat the competition because we

consider market share, sales volume, or any other metric more important than the Governing Objective.'

- Decisions based on execution bias. This is the desire to be seen acting with a bias towards intuition and experience. Such decision-makers are afraid of having to build a factbase because it might contradict their own entrenched opinions.

The common denominator in all of the above is reactivity, in which mental conditioning drives decision-making without conscious effort. In other words, such decisions are made on autopilot without any real intelligent input. No doubt some of these decisions might eventually turn out to be correct – but that's purely a bet! Running a company on a gamble is not a good idea.

There are many examples in the corporate world in which such automatic decision-making has led to value destruction. Some examples from our own experience include:

- Matching the competitors' pricing without due consideration for value.
- Orchestrating a big acquisition in pursuit of building an empire despite it being value-destroying (scale for scale's sake).
- Selling products for fear of missing out, without regard for customers' needs and treating them fairly.
- Following competitors down the risk curve in a very hot market – and paying for it later.

Principles

In our opinion, there are four key principles involved in effective decision-making. The first three principles aim to optimise the decision-making process and decouple the mental conditioning of the decision-maker from the decision itself. The fourth principle is a check to ensure that the decision-making process does not ignore important but missing information. Ideally, these four should all be in play when facing decisions of strategic importance.

1. Decisions must be based on Facts. This sounds obvious, yet so many decision-makers ignore this simple guideline. There are many examples where important strategic decisions were made based on feelings rather than facts. This principle forces you to go out and collect the facts. It is important at this

stage not to make the decision and then go out and collect only the facts that support it but to remain open-minded as to all the facts that are relevant. In this domain, we define the word 'fact' very broadly. On the one hand, it could be a set of quantitative and qualitative data either from the past or today; on the other hand, it could be a set of hypotheses about the future underpinned by the best set of 'data' available. In either case, the point of principle is that the collection of an articulated factbase supports better dialogues and the generation of Alternatives (see below).

2. Decisions must be made from a set of Alternatives. One should make an effort to study all the available Alternatives. Good Alternatives are meaningfully different from each other and are coherent and credible. The better the alternatives, the better the outcome of the decision-making process. One should not under-estimate the effort that goes into generating a credible set of Alternatives.

Decision-making that involves identifying and evaluating multiple Alternatives before making a decision can help significantly reduce the potential cognitive biases in the final decision because it forces you to consider multiple options and viewpoints rather than just relying on your initial gut reaction or preconceived notions.

By considering a complete set of Alternatives, you are more likely to be exposed to new information and perspectives that may challenge your initial assumptions or biases. This can help you avoid making decisions based on incomplete or distorted information and instead make decisions based on a more balanced and objective evaluation of the available alternatives.

3. Decisions must be derived from the set of available alternatives using specific Decision Rules. This is really a simple economic optimisation problem: maximise the Governing Objective subject to a set of constraints. The whole process can be easily described as a series of questions. The first question is invariably:

- Which is the most value-creating Alternative?

The second question is also straightforward:

- Are the Alternatives in alignment with the company's Vision (Purpose and Values)?

If, for example, the most value-creating Alternative is not in alignment with either the Purpose of the company or its Values, then it should be discarded for the second most valuable one, etc. This sounds obvious, but articulating Decision Rules will spare a lot of unnecessary discussions in the Boardroom.

The subsequent set of Decision Rules depend on the specific company and the industry in which it operates. For example, a set of Decision Rules might look like:

- Does the Alternative support the shape of the financial forecast acceptable to investors?
- Does the Alternative support fair customer outcomes?
- Does the Alternative support fair ESG outcomes?
- Does the Alternative align with the acceptable Risk Appetite?

The complete set of Decision Rules are also called Sustainability Tests because their application ensures that value created for the company owners is sustained over the long term and does not come at the expense of customers, colleagues, the community, or the destruction of the environment.

4. Decisions must be supported by the intuition of decision-maker(s). Notice that this principle comes last, not first. The reason is that many people tend to confuse their intuition with their mental conditioning, which shortcuts conscious decision-making for automatic choice.

Our definition of intuition in this context is data patterns in our memory which we recognise on a sub-conscious level without having conscious access to the core data itself. So, intuition is not something irrational or mysterious. Rather, it is active pattern recognition, which sends us a strong or even knowing feeling about something without having recourse to the data itself. Usually, we become alarmed when something feels wrong without knowing why. Therefore, intuition should never ever be disregarded. That is also why facts and intuition always go hand in hand. Relying exclusively on one without the help of the other reinforces the decisioning gamble.

As such, we always recommend checking whether you intuitively trust the decision that you're about to make. If something is telling you not to, then return to fact-finding and generating alternatives. Have the courage to keep looking for those hidden data points that trigger your intuition, and don't move forward until you find out what they are.

Since intuition is deeply personal, it cannot be operationalised in the context of collective decision-making in bodies such as the company Board or the ExCo. Hence, it is up to the Chairman of the decision-making body to test the intuition of the participants.

It is important to note that uncertainty inherent in any decision cannot be eliminated entirely. The purpose of these four principles is not to eliminate the uncertainty but to eliminate the wrong reasons as to why decisions are made, as well as to optimise the mechanistic approach to the decision-making process.

Actions

In this case, the actions one can take to make better decisions follow the above principles closely.

1. Build a factbase. Facts will give you the foundations of a decision and will eliminate a lot of the decision-making gamble. Build a deep quantitative and qualitative factbase – think back to the 'poet and mathematician' philosophy. Ground the facts in detailed and granular economics (EP and EV). Study where your company/business unit is creating and losing value against the competition:

- Products/Customers/Channels/Geographies
- Customer Offer/Value Proposition
- Cost/Operating Position
- Pricing

2. Create a set of alternatives.

- Ask yourself, 'What are the alternatives?' and build a complete set – not just the obvious ones.
- Make the alternatives coherent and meaningfully different from one another.
- Postpone judgement about whether any alternative is realistic or unrealistic, good or bad; 'suspend judgement' and be open to anything (in our experience, a good meeting chair can set the tone

here). Remember, Decision Rules bring discipline to the judgement process.

3. Apply the decision rules.

- Which alternative maximises sustainable long-term Owner Value subject to a set of conditions (Sustainability Tests)?
- Sometimes at this stage, one might have to pivot back to redefine the set of available alternatives or even go back to fact-finding.

4. Check whether you intuitively trust the decision that you're about to make. If something tells you 'no', then pivot back to fact-finding and generating alternatives again.

Even for the big strategic choices facing every company, this process does not have to take long. What is important is eliminating any inherent biases from all decision-makers around the table.

This type of decision-making process is also applicable to a whole host of smaller decisions in the corporate context, e.g., sorting out a conflict between two people on your team or figuring out whether someone deserves to keep their job.

Potential Pitfalls

One cannot expect to become good at this decision-making process overnight. Effective decision-making is a skill, and we all need to spend time practising it.

Frequently, those with an 'execution' or 'over-confidence' bias will try to circumvent good decision-making. It is critical that the CEO has the courage to allow the process to follow its natural course and allow all participants to debate the facts and alternatives. Ego, power, and position, if unchecked and abused, are the enemy of good decision-making.

Often, one will be tempted to shortcut the process. Fear, conditioning, and the desire to please everyone are very powerful sub-conscious motivators. One must always bear this in mind and remind oneself why this process is applied in the first place.

All big corporate failures can be traced to the absence of an effective decision-making process. The leaders either did not know the facts, did not study the alternatives, or completely ignored the intuition of someone on the team.

7. Customer Value: How to Focus on Your Customers

Issue: Customer centricity without due concern for the Governing Objective is a recipe for disaster.

Many Board members and managers around the executive table, both experienced and inexperienced, take great pride in being customer advocates. Unfortunately, they often forget that satisfying customer needs must also produce sustainable value for owners; otherwise, the company's competitiveness will become unsustainable. Being focused on the customer should not, and cannot, preclude maximising sustainable Owner Value.

For example, we have both worked with colleagues who were vocal and relentless in their advocacy for customers. For these colleagues, customer needs and wants were sacrosanct. Unfortunately, the concept of Customer Value and its relationship to Owner Value was completely alien. No matter how hard we tried to explain it, their views were entrenched. The logic was simple: 'I care about the customers, and if we all do so, profit will follow.' This is what we came to call 'misplaced customer centricity' – which we will explain later. This view of the world created real tension and conflict, reduced the overall effectiveness of the team, and created a culture of 'passive aggression' towards the Governing Objective and the integrity of the Blueprint (Governing Objective, Vision, and Management Model).We have found that many managers also commit a second grave mistake: they measure customer profitability like they measure company profitability – on a yearly basis. This can be very misleading as Customer Value is often generated following the initial cost of acquisition. The best approach is to measure Customer Value on a lifetime basis, although this, too, is fraught with potential challenges.

A suitable example of why it is not good enough to measure customer profitability on a single-period basis can be found in Retail Banking. Consider a simple mortgage as a product. If we were to measure the profitability of a mortgage in the first year only, it would most probably be loss-making because there is usually a significant cost of acquisition in terms of marketing costs or intermediary commissions. Mortgages are multi-year products, and the initial loss can only be recouped in later years. It simply cannot be looked at through a single-year lens. This is obvious for mortgages, but if you think about it, it is true for any product, even groceries; if your customer experience in the grocery store is pleasant enough and the price is right, it can result in multiple purchases year after year.

Principles

There are a number of principles that must be applied:

1. Maximising Owners' Value and creating Customer Value are not mutually exclusive, although it can appear that way to many colleagues. Whenever there is a conflict between the two, the Governing Objective must take precedence (see Chapter 1 as to why). Any other choice will eventually undermine the viability of the company's business model.

2. Total Customer Value has two components: 'Value To' and 'Value From' the Customer.[4]

- 'Value To' Customer = All the benefits and satisfaction that customers derive from a product/service minus the price they have paid for this product/service.
- 'Value From' Customer = The price that the company charges the customer for their product/service less the company's total economic cost to serve this product/service.

Clearly it is a mistake to consider only 'Value To' and ignore the 'Value From' dimension. This gives rise to the so-called 'misplaced customer centricity',

---

[4] M. Blanco, and R. Langford, 'Sales Force Effectiveness: How to Balance Customer Centricity and Shareholder Value', *Marakon Commentary*, June 2017.

where we care about customer benefits but ignore the sustainability of the company. It's also a mistake to think only about 'Value From', as this will in turn negate management's understanding of customer needs and wants, which will also lead to undermining the company's viability.

Undoubtedly, both elements of Customer Value are equally important, which means that management needs to be able to measure on a lifetime basis.

3. Mot all customers are equal. In our experience, a material proportion of customers are not economically viable at any point in time and need a bespoke offer. Without this information, pursuing the Governing Objective becomes untenable.

Actions

Some of the key actions that leaders should consider for managing Customer Value include:[5]

1. Measuring 'Value From': In most practical cases, one can use simple metrics. Many companies often commit the mistake of trying to perform an exact measurement, which can bog them down in measuring exercises. There is usually no need for exact precision to reach the right conclusion as to which customer segments are economically viable. Implementing economic segmentation by using value metrics such as EP (over a single period) and EV (over customer relationship lifetime) to find out which customers to keep, which to offer a different proposition, and which to exit is key.

2. Measuring 'Value To': To quantify this, the company should survey its customers to gauge their satisfaction and whether their expectations are being met. Net Promoter Score®, created by Bain & Company, is one such methodology that we have successfully used in the past. It is advisable to complement a primary approach with behavioural and demographic segmentation, e.g., studying customers' needs, wants, and behaviours for marketing purposes.

---

[5] Et al.

3. Linking Reward to Outcomes: Management must also link sales performance to both 'Value From' and 'Value To' customers while meeting regulatory requirements and meeting the principles of Reward in Chapter 7.

Potential Pitfalls

There are a number of pitfalls that must be avoided:

1. New Customers vs. Existing Customers. New and existing customers are very different in terms of both needs and value. There is a lot of contention about whether one should, and indeed could, offer the same price to both groups. In our experience, differentiated pricing is based on point-in-time cost of acquisition and risk propensity – which will change over time and at any point in time. The bottom line is that all pricing should be underpinned by 'Value From' and 'Value To' – if either cannot be met (at any point in time), then a different proposition needs to be developed. This subject is a landmine in certain industries like banking and insurance.

2. Capability Gaps. Applying the principles above requires developing some specific capabilities. A lack of the following capabilities can stop you in your tracks when attempting to manage Customer Value effectively:

- Customer segmentation capability – segmentation based on lifetime value, risk, demographics, and behaviours is an absolute must.
- Product design capability – creating products that satisfy customers' needs and provide a superior customer experience.
- Pricing management capability – measuring price elasticity and simulating price/volume scenarios.
- Competitor intelligence capability – this generally regards how the competitors are handling all of the above.

8. Investor Relations: How to Be Good at It

Issue: The company valuation modelled by investors often differs from that of the company directors, which can create asymmetry issues between the two parties.

The information asymmetry between company insiders (such as directors) and outsiders (such as investors) creates a gap between the intrinsic and extrinsic valuation of the company. This is often a problem in large, publicly listed companies or companies in which the owners and managers are different sets of people.

Management's information is always more complete than that of investors. Some of this information asymmetry includes projects and initiatives that cannot be communicated directly without risking the company's competitive position. Hence, a value gap is always going to be in play, where the extrinsic valuation lags behind the intrinsic over time or vice versa.

Therefore, the role of an effective Investor Relations (IR) function is to:

- Reduce the information gap between Investors and Directors without disclosing sensitive competitive information, thereby reducing the valuation gap over time.
- Ensure compliance with Stock Exchange regulations and other legal requirements.
- Create a communication bridge between Investors and Directors by acting as an interface between the company and investors/industry

analysts, ensuring that the investors' voice is heard internally and vice versa.

In other words, IR helps investors make the right decisions by sharing key information within legal and regulatory requirements. Without an effective IR function, the information gap between Management and Investors is only going to grow larger over time due to informational entropy.

This places a unique set of requirements on those who work in IR. They must be equally fluent and comfortable in communicating the company's strategy in the context of the big picture and in discussing broad and deep financial and regulatory reporting specifics with external analysts.

Principles

As always, there are several key principles that need to be applied to maximise the effectiveness of the IR functions.

Financial and Valuation Literacy

It is critical that ExCo and the Board review and sign off on the intrinsic value of the company (on both an overall and value-per-share basis) at half and full year. This is another reason why the integrated strategic and financial planning process must be embedded into the company's DNA.

As we discussed earlier, the intrinsic value of the company is the sum of the invested equity plus the sum of discounted economic profits over the planning, transition, and steady-state periods (classic corporate finance DCF valuation).

The intrinsic valuation per share must then be compared to the present and targeted share price of the company (as communicated by equity analysts). This will then indicate whether the company is under or overvalued – and, most importantly, shape the IR messages to investors.

In terms of messaging, it is critical that IR provide 'guidance' and not 'targets' as management must have the space to pivot its strategic direction based on new and emerging facts.

Transparency

Investor Relations is, at its heart, about sharing information that investors need to create an informed valuation of the company. This includes all information specifically required by Stock Exchange regulations as well as addressing any bad news head-on, even if it triggers a fall in the share price. It does not, however, include any commercially sensitive information that might jeopardise the company's competitive position.

Being completely transparent with investors in both good times and bad times builds trust, even if the share price drops in the short term. This way, investors know that the information gap between them and the company is always kept to a minimum.

Consistency

This is about sharing the same information with all investors regardless of their size or influence over the company. In addition, it means always addressing any gaps between what you have said before and what you are saying in the present. That is, the Value Story must remain dynamic but be communicated consistently.

Compliance

This is about ensuring that all information shared with investors is compliant with all laws and guidelines. This includes financial reporting, market disclosures, dealing with price-sensitive information, listing obligations, treatment of inside information, M&A transactions regulations, etc. IR compliance mistakes are usually very costly for the company – both in monetary and reputational terms.

Visibility

This is about being visible and available to investors/industry analysts. Effective IR ensures that the investors' voice is heard in the company as much as the company's voice is heard in the investor and the analyst community.

By adhering to these principles, one should expect the following:

- Convergence of extrinsic and intrinsic valuations over time. Of course, there is always going to be a gap, but it would trend down over time.

- Less share price shocks from short-term results fluctuations due to the consistency of the company's Value Story.
- Increased level of trust between the company and investors. After all, long-term value does imply long-term relationships with investors.
- Lower cost of capital as the investor community understands the business better and the unavoidable information gap is kept smaller.

Actions

Create a Compelling Value Story

The Value Story is about how the company intends to create value for its shareholders/investors over time. It articulates the long-term strategy of the company. This way, investors' attention will be consistently focused on the long term.

The Value Story must be articulated in both non-financial and financial terms. Non-financially, it should include the company's market participation strategy, its competitive strategy, and a selected list of initiatives of how it is to create value for its owners. It should be supported by long-term industry-specific financial commitments, which reflect the way industry analysts look at the market. That said, we must confess that we have a strong bias towards value measures, such as TSR.[6] The Value Story must be easy to express in any setting, e.g., an investor conference or a private meeting, using language which investors understand.

It is also possible to create an internal version of the Value Story. This would be the same as the external version, except for management being able to share additional, commercially sensitive information that cannot otherwise be disseminated freely outside of the company. This internal Value Story can then be used in all strategy meetings and financial results communications with colleagues.

---

[6] Total Shareholder Returns. See Chapter 9 for why this is the most important external value measure for any company.

Embed the Value Story

Over time, the Value Story must be deeply embedded in all communications with investors, analysts, and any other external parties interested in the company's performance. The CEO, CFO, and the Head of IR should not hesitate to repeat the Value Story at every opportunity. This will help focus investor attention on both short- and long-term performance.

Furthermore, every company executive must know and be able to tell the Value Story. This way, the IR message's reach will be greatly expanded.

Reduce the Information Gap

At every opportunity, including at each results announcement call, the CEO and the CFO must, without exception, create a bridge between the current financial results of the company and the long-term Value Story. In other words, they must illustrate clearly to investors where the company is on its Value Story journey. This will help investors update their valuations and consider the long-term effects of the short-term results within the context provided by the company. The principles of Transparency and Consistency must be applied without exception to nourish the relationship of trust between the parties.

In addition to the financial information required by law, IR should also consider sharing certain non-financial information, such as:

- The Governing Objective (and its associated Value Goals)
- The Company's Vision (Purpose, Values, Behaviours, or even Operating Manners)
- The Key Elements of the Management Model (such as its Decision-Making or Strategic Management Process)
- The Key Elements of its factbase (such as market share or share of market value)

The availability of such information will help investors create an informed view as to how the company is managed and reduce the investment risk that they associate with it.

Finally, IR should continuously transmit information both ways between company executives and investors/industry analysts. This will help executives understand investors' thinking, which is critical; otherwise, they are prone to fundamental errors like misunderstanding 'customer centricity' (see Chapter 7).

Create an IR Calendar

Setting an IR Operating Rhythm in sync with the broader corporate Operating Rhythm is an important element of the Consistency principle above. It should be relatively easy to plan a whole year of investor interactions, from results announcements to investor conferences. The IR calendar should also include time for proactive engagement with investors.

Potential Pitfalls

Educating the company executives about investors' expectations is just as important as informing the investors about the company's performance and Value Story. We have met many executives who are excellent at their functional jobs and Board members who provide valuable check and challenge but are ill-informed and inexperienced as to how investors think and how the capital markets operate. This is a key risk to any IR strategy and must be specifically addressed by the company. It is also a fundamental risk to the effective performance of an ExCo and Board and something that must be faced head-on by both CEO and Chairman. Indeed, we would go as far as to say that this is a fundamental performance management or development issue that must be seen as a minimum standard. In our opinion, without this 'minimum standard', both the Board and ExCo do not pass muster. In simple terms, the authors believe that a deep understanding of value and the capital markets is a minimum standard for any senior executive or Board member.

Using external measures to manage internal performance and make decisions is a mistake that many companies commit when they are too eager to address investor expectations. Inevitably, the CFO is the biggest culprit, so they must be fluent in both sides of the coin; that is, able to distinguish between market measures (e.g., RoE, EPS, and P/E) that do not support the Governing Objective, strategy development and resource allocation, and internal measures (EP and EV), which are integral to a high-performing organisation. Again, we believe that a CFO who is not fluent in both languages is only 'half-cooked' and must be developed. Any resistance or silent disagreement must be managed head-on (see Chapter 26).

Viewing IR as a highly specialised function that adds no value to the company's operations is another pitfall that some executives fall into. Investor Relations is not just the job of the CEO, CFO, and IR team. It's everyone's job to know and repeat the Value Story at every opportunity.

9. Value Creation: How to Measure It

Issue: Most companies do not use any KPIs that measure short- or long-term value creation.

Many books have been written on KPIs and measuring performance, so we don't want to overwhelm you here. We would just like to point out some of the key principles that can help guide your thinking in the context of maximising value for your company's owners over time – after all, that is the Governing Objective of any business with an equity base.

Measuring value creation (or destruction) is important for companies because it will provide a guide as to whether they are achieving their Governing Objective. Without proper value metrics, it is also impossible to support effective decision-making, strategy development, and resource allocation. Furthermore, as we mentioned previously, even if they don't ever admit it, there are too many corporate executives who manage companies using market KPIs such as RoE, EPS, or P/E ratio, focus on quarterly and annual results, and essentially respond to external pressures. Such metrics are useful in an Investor Relations / external reporting context – as they allow investors to compare companies in the same sector – but they are tragically deficient for effective decision-making, strategy development, and resources. We cannot stress enough how using market measures to run a company's internal processes – such as strategy development and resource allocation – is flawed.

In addition, managing for short-term results is a recipe for disaster. For starters, it always leads to chronic underinvestment. This, in turn, damages the long-term prospects of any company as it precludes capability building, delays investments in value-creating strategies, cuts down on R&D, etc. The cost base is kept low, but so is investment in future growth. Of course, the investment case must be fact-based, alternatives-driven, and subject to a detailed risk-return analysis.

Furthermore, the lack of value measures means that many companies, even very profitable ones, do not know with certainty where the value they are creating is coming from or whether they truly maximised the sustainable value for their owners. For example, they might consider their whole customer base to be profitable, while clearly not all customers will be the same. This could lead to a strategy of maximising market share, which can unwittingly lead to value destruction.

Principles

Value Metrics Are Inexorably Linked to Strategic Performance

Value metrics are indispensable for:

- Formulating and evaluating strategy alternatives (see Chapter 3 and Chapter 6)
- Allocating resources (most importantly, owners' capital)
- Measuring economic profitability across the portfolio of products, channels, customers, geographies, etc.
- Prioritising within the Management Agenda (see Chapter 3)
- Evaluating and managing performance against the Governing Objective and the company's Value Goals (see Chapter 3)
- Any other management decisions that involve the delivery of the company's Governing Objective

This gives value metrics a strategic dominance over other KPIs, which could be financial, operational, regulatory, organisational, marketing, HR, and so on.

Internal Value Metrics

In our experience, the best internal measures of value are EP and EV. They both measure value creation (or destruction) by incorporating the cost of invested capital in the company's profitability calculations. Adding the cost of capital to the cost base reflects the true economic cost of delivering a product or service.

Economic Profit

EP can be used to measure value creation (i.e., economic profitability):

Economic Profit (EP) = 'Earnings After Tax' – 'Cost of Invested Capital

Alternatively,

EP = ('Return on Equity' – 'Cost of Equity') x 'Invested Equity

It can be used to measure value creation (i.e., economic profitability) per product, per customer segment, per channel, per business unit, etc. It could be both backward- and forward-looking, which means it can be used both for forecasting future performance and managing past performance. Most importantly, EP is a single-period measure, and it is not suitable for measuring value creation over multiple reporting periods.

Economic Value

EV is the value creation measure to use over multiple reporting periods:

Economic Value (EV) = Invested Equity + Present Value of Future EP

Corporate strategy, allocation of resources, Management Agenda initiatives, and many financial products such as mortgages all span multiple years; therefore, EV is the best metric to measure expected value creation over time. EV is usually a forward-looking measure, but it could also be used retrospectively for performance management when a more accurate market-based measure is unavailable.

External Value Metrics

The most effective market-based measure for retrospective value creation is TSR.

Total Shareholder Return = Share Price Appreciation + Dividend Yield (both over the same period).

TSR is a market-based measure that can be readily calculated from Stock Exchange data. It is backwards-looking and measures long-term value creation for shareholders. This makes it ideal for performance management purposes, such as corporate LTIPs. Unfortunately, it is only available for publicly quoted companies.

Relative Metrics Are Better Than Absolute Metrics

When estimating value creation, it is always a good idea to use relative measures. Very often, a company might have over-performed against its original plan but, in fact, under-performed against the competition. This will indicate very strongly that management missed an opportunity for better performance, which must be considered during the Performance Management process (see Chapter 22).

Economic profitability of customer segments, distribution channels, business units, or geographies should also always be done on a relative basis to inform better decisions.

Value Metrics Do Not Require 100 Per Cent Accuracy

It is worth noting that complete accuracy of EP and EV is not required to support effective decision-making. Complete accuracy could be very costly and time-consuming to achieve. That is, the marginal gains from extra accuracy cannot compensate for the marginal cost of achieving it. Moreover, if these value measures are used on a relative basis (e.g., customer segment vs. another) as recommended above, complete accuracy is also not required.

Allocations of invested capital and fixed costs are usually the most challenging, yet they can always be approximated by using an appropriate value driver.

Actions

There are a number of actions that could be considered:

1. Embed value metrics (EP, EV, and TSR) in the company's Management Model. The above value metrics are essential for any company that chooses a Governing Objective of maximising value to the shareholders over time. The most important Management Model processes, such as decision-making, Management Agenda prioritisation, and performance management, depend on these metrics.

In our experience, implementing value metrics is more of a cultural issue than a technical or management reporting issue. The problem is not with the metrics per se but with their implications. Very often, value metrics directly challenge some of the deep beliefs and convictions of incumbent executives, such as 'the balanced scorecard', 'all customers are valuable', 'growing market share as a top objective', 'RoE is the only measure for shareholders', etc. It is critical that the metrics become mandatory and are endorsed by key ExCo members, in particular, the CFO. We would go so far as to say that resistance or silent dissent from the CFO or Finance team is one of the biggest challenges for the CEO in embedding the Management Model and should be a focus of recruitment, selection, and performance management. CEO/CFO alignment on all elements of the Blueprint is non-negotiable.

2. Understand what drives value creation (or destruction) in your company and focus on those levers. For example, if you focus on Customer Value, it can be analysed into 'Value To' and 'Value From'. The key drivers of 'Value To' customers could include certain service features that you offer and at what cost. On the other hand, the driver of 'Value From' customers will include the price they are willing to pay for these features and the volume they are willing to buy (see Chapter 7 for more details.) In addition, further breaking down customers by segments (behavioural, demographic, or other) could shed further light on where the value is coming from.

A similar analysis can be conducted by product or service, channel, business unit, or by Geography.

3. Use value metrics to change the dialogue with investors. In our experience, investors respect companies that use value metrics to make

decisions. Multi-period value metrics, such as EV and TSR, can help shift the investors' focus from the short term to the long term. Despite some fluctuations that might occur in the short term, if the Value Story (see Chapter 8) remains intact, investors might not react as they otherwise would toward negative news.

Management should be routinely comparing the intrinsic valuation of the company to the investors' valuation (i.e., the share price), figure out where they differ, and iterate the Value Story.

Potential Pitfalls

We have already mentioned that value metrics have the potential to challenge certain deep and long-held beliefs held by key decision-makers. Giving in to their resistance and silent disagreement are potential pitfalls that you must be aware of.

Another important pitfall to avoid is the search for 100 per cent accuracy of these measures. Measuring product, customer, or channel value with complete accuracy could be very costly and delay decision-making for a long time – and be used as an excuse to abandon the measures entirely.

SECTION 2: SHAPING THE ORGANISATION

The Organisational Blueprint (Governing Objective, Vision, and Management Model) sets boundaries and associated processes for how any company should be led and managed. This section is about setting the structures upon which the Blueprint can be delivered. Section 2 is organised as follows:

Chapter 10 addresses the issue of setting an Organisational Structure in support of strategy development and implementation. There are too many companies operating on an outdated Organisational Structure that is often a legacy of past mergers and acquisitions or other historical events. These structures often impede the company's capability to execute its chosen strategy. Therefore, designing an Organisational Structure that is aligned with and supports the delivery of the company's strategy is critical.

Chapter 11 discusses Organisational Culture. Culture in many companies is often quite rigid and is often seen as an impediment to change. Creating a culture that enables and supports change is a key requirement for producing outstanding results.

Chapter 12 discusses establishing a corporate Operating Rhythm. Every company operates in many different cycles, and synchronising these cycles will improve organisational efficiency and effectiveness while also setting the ground for high performance.

Chapter 13 addresses the issue of effective Corporate Communications. Everything that happens in a company depends on people. Hence their ability to communicate with each other effectively is critical in any high-performing company. Means of communication can take many forms – conversations, emails, instant messaging, presentations, etc. – and yet the principles of effective communication are always the same.

Chapter 14 is dedicated to conducting effective meetings. Huge amounts of time are wasted in corporate meetings that never seem to achieve the intentions of their organisers. As a result, meetings have developed a bad reputation in many companies. Yet the problem is not the meetings themselves but the unproductive use of time.

Finally, **Chapter 15** is dedicated to the use of external consultants. Many companies routinely become over-dependent on external consultants. This brings along several negative consequences – most notably, capability deficiency in many functional areas. Consultants have their rightful place in business, but they must only be used in specific situations and subject to specific principles.

10. Structure: How to Set an Effective Organisational Structure

Issue: The Organisational Structure of many companies is not aligned with their Strategy as well as it should be.

In many companies, Organisational Structure is often quite outdated. This might seem strange, but changing the structure is generally met with a lot of resistance in any organisation. People grow attached to their teams, their departments and, often, their own titles. When a new CEO comes in, they tend to reshuffle the structure; however, this rarely links to changes in Strategy. In a vast number of companies, the Organisational Structure is a result of many years of tinkering to accommodate for:

- Capabilities of specific individuals
- Entries into new product or service markets
- Mergers or acquisitions

Therefore, such Organisational Structures are often based on several compromises. For smaller companies (say, based in only one country), such compromises result in overly complex structures, while in large multinationals, the result is complicated matrix structures, which are often impossible to manage effectively. Consequently, such structures often hinder both the delivery of the Strategy and the correct distribution of accountability amongst senior executives and managers.

For example, in many large PLCs, the drive for scale for its own sake (or sometimes the drive to build personal empires) leads to large, unmanageable business units where businesses are banged together on a whim without any thought for line of sight to performance or accountability.

Principles

There are a number of principles that must be applied:

1. The Organisational Structure of any company must logically support its Strategy. It's a mistake to do it the other way around. The Organisational Design must be reviewed or changed by the CEO and the Board as often as they review or change the company Strategy. Indeed, Structure must be viewed as the very first item on the Management Agenda after the Strategy is defined.

2. There are three key building blocks to any Organisational Structure: (i) SBUs, (ii) Specialist Support Functions, and (iii) Scale Support Functions:

- SBUs must be organised around the main value-creating centres. SBUs could have various dimensions (such as Product/Service Market, Customer Segment, Distribution Channel, or Geography). Yet, there must always be a primary dimension, as shaped by strategic choices, to ensure management accountability is defined beyond doubt.

- Specialist Support Functions (SSFs) are the organisational units that provide specialist activity for SBUs; for example, S&P, Corporate Development, Legal, Procurement, and Tax.

- Scale Support Functions provide both specialist resources and economies of scale and scope for what we might call 'scale daily operational activity'. We might also call these functions Shared Service Units.

3. Structure is the main vehicle through which accountability is distributed across the organisation to executives and managers. In this regard, we hold views that are counter-intuitive and, indeed, an anathema to many (including, in our experience, the CFO and private investors!). In our experience and opinion, when designing the Organisational Structure, it is always constructive to start with the premise that the benefits of duplication outweigh the costs if that reinforces line of sight, performance accountability, and ownership. It is critically important not to assume automatically that economies of scale are

justified only on an efficiency basis if putting all functional activities together blurs performance measurement. Therefore, very often, the benefits of duplication – through ownership and accountability – outweigh the benefits of economies of scale.

As mentioned above, this is counter-intuitive to many senior executives, whose natural disposition is to put all functional activities together and eliminate all duplication in the search for 'cost out'; however, the driver of such a decision must always remain long-term value creation and not efficiency alone. Because it is much harder to prove the revenue side of this value equation than the cost side, we have found that starting with this premise creates the right debate around the ExCo table. The key question then becomes 'Why should the resources/activities not be in the SBU?' vs. the often default question of 'Why shouldn't resources be centralised?'

4. The span of control should not exceed seven to ten direct reports at every level of the organisation. A lower number is better than a higher number, but it is not always strategically practical.

Actions

There are a number of actions that could be considered:

1. It is often easier to begin with the Specialist SFs. The SSFs have two main responsibilities: (i) they set (and enforce) the standards in their specialist area, and (ii) they provide associated services to SBUs. Large companies may consider splitting these two responsibilities in two: one branch in the Group Centre, which sets the standards, and another branch in each of the SBUs, which provide the services. Keeping the Group Centre as small as possible allows the SBUs to have their own Support Function teams and ignores the clamour for large, integrated functions (decision-making should rest in the hands of SBU MDs). At a minimum, every organisation must have:

- Finance
- HR
- Strategy & Planning
- Legal

Leading Without Winging It

It might be that size necessitates that a 'functional shared services' model where dual-solid reporting must be accepted; however, in this case, the sacrosanct principle is that strategy development, strategy execution, performance accountability (for both revenue and cost) and 'leading' must be in the hands of those nearest the customer (however defined).

In many companies (banks in particular), there are two special kinds of Specialist Support Functions, whose purpose is to protect the company from various external and internal risks:

- Risk Management, including Compliance (the 'Second Line of Defence')
- Internal Audit (the 'Third Line of Defence')

2. Define the Scale SFs whose role is to provide large-scale activities – and set standards – in an efficient and effective manner under Service Level Agreements to the SBUs.

Even though our default position is to place as much resource and accountability as possible into the hands of SBU managing directors in accordance with the principles above (even if there's a level of duplication across functional activity), there still could be a few specialist activity areas where economies of scale and scope are justified, and, most importantly, part of the company Strategy. For example, it is plausible to assume that shared IT infrastructure is one of those legitimate group-scale resources.

The CEO should make the SBU MDs feel accountable for running their business by exposing them to the vagaries of income and cost management, subject to the standards set by the Group Centre.

3. Define the key SBUs, i.e., the centre of activity where value is generated. The best way to approach this is by referring to the Strategy and the underlying factbase. For example:

- If the main value generated in the Strategy is based on geographical regions, then SBUs could be defined as geographies, e.g., UK, EU, Americas, Asia, etc.
- If product diversification, then product based SBUs (loans, deposits, mortgages in banking)

- If customer-centric, then customer based SBUs (retail, wholesale, SME, or large corporates)
- If distribution channel, then channel based SBUs (online, mobile, branch, etc)

In any event, strive to make the SBUs feel like end-to-end enterprises with clear accountabilities, decision rights, and reporting lines. Create 'mini-CEO' roles but never label as them as 'CEO'; there is only ever one CEO whose reporting line is to the Group Chairman.

4. Finally, in our experience, the role of CTO could be very valuable for companies. The CTO should partner up with the CSO to create a balance between 'doing' and high-quality 'thinking'. In general, the CTO would:

- Be the keeper of the Management Agenda
- Track progress across all the initiatives as well as all other commitments on behalf of the CEO
- Initiate corrective actions

Potential Pitfalls

If the Organisational Structure is not reviewed when the Strategy changes, the implementation of the Strategy is hindered. Whenever the Strategy changes, the CEO and the Board must review the Structure and assess if it is providing adequate support.

If the Organisational Structure changes more often than the Strategy, then this could be a source of confusion in the organisation. There are some CEOs and senior executives who love to play with Organisational Design. They are addicted to structural changes because it feeds their need for control and domination. This is also a mistake because every company needs a period of stability to execute its Strategy. By the way, the same argument applies to the company's Strategy. It should not be changed fundamentally too often.

Cases when roles are created to fit the skillsets of specific individuals rather than to reflect the Strategy of the organisation can lead to silent disagreement or even contempt. While this could be justified in some cases, the justification must be solid for a rare talent and should never be a recurring practice or policy of the organisation.

When roles are created to feed the egos of specific individuals this is another potentially explosive issue. Empire builders are very common in the corporate world, and the Board and the CEO should avoid this at all costs.

Overly complex matrix structures can often inhibit the implementation of the Strategy. Such structures always imply dual accountabilities, which itself is very difficult to manage. Where possible, they should be avoided.

Another pitfall to avoid is when the drive for efficiency (cost savings) is mistakenly seen as the value-maximising approach. Unless this is the stated Strategy of the organisation, this is a fallacy. The key relationship is between accountability and value creation. The default position must be to set up the SBUs around the dominant value-creating dimension and then allow general managers to set strategy and deliver results by owning as many of the resources as possible.

The cost base of the organisation can get out of hand if the Heads of Functions are not incentivised to support value maximisation. The Integrated Planning Process must ensure the Functions are providing their services to the rest of the organisation in both an efficient and effective manner. The CEO must ensure that value for money is being provided and keep a watchful eye over HR and Risk and Compliance, in particular, where the former sometimes struggle to contain cost growth, and the latter can stand behind the Regulator as a means of gaming resource allocation.

11. Culture: How to Use Organisational Culture to Facilitate Change

Issue: Organisational Culture is often seen as an impediment to change, but it does not have to be.

In a corporate context, the word 'culture' is often employed as an amorphous, all-encompassing concept that is used to explain various behaviours at all levels of an organisation. Everyone discusses culture freely, but when they are hard-pressed to provide a definition, it proves difficult. There are many definitions of Organisational Culture floating around, and many management academics have written about it. In this respect, the subject of Organisational Culture is like the subject of Corporate Strategy – there are many people who think they are experts because the subject seems intuitively appealing.

Here are a couple of classical definitions. Schein (1992) defines culture as 'A pattern of shared basic assumptions that the group learnt as it solved its problems of external adaptation and internal integration, and that have worked well enough to be considered valid…'[7] Sorensen (2002) defines it as the '…complex set of values, beliefs, philosophies and symbols that characterises the way in which a firm conducts its business'.[8] The challenge that pragmatic leaders have with both definitions is how to apply them when leading. We will come back to this later in the chapter.

---

[7] Edgard Shein, *Organizational Culture and Leadership*, Wiley; 5th edition, 2016.
[8] J.B. Sorensen, 'The Strength of Corporate Culture and the Reliability of Firm Performance' *Administrative Science Quarterly*, 47, 2002.

The reality is that many leaders are ill-equipped to handle cultural issues in their organisations. They know how to get things done, but cultural change appears impossible to achieve through managerial action alone. For that reason, many managers, especially in large corporations, experience culture as something given. It is a large immovable background that requires enormous effort to bend to their will. At best, they perceive culture as a set of constraints within which they can operate; at worst, they perceive it as a major barrier to change.

To make things worse, the culture in many companies has developed more by accident than by design. For example, there are many companies around the world in which the person at the helm is seen as an omniscient presence by both employees and the larger public. Although in the 20th century it was possible to have an all-knowing, all-capable, very talented person at the top and be a successful company at the same time, in the age of digital technology and artificial intelligence, this type of culture is quickly becoming untenable and risky.

Finally, looking from the outside in, it is very tempting to attribute a particular company's apparent success to its 'culture'. The theory of competitive advantage tells us that if the source of advantage is difficult to imitate, then it can be enjoyed for a very long time. Unfortunately, culture as a source of competitive advantage is difficult to create because it does not easily lend itself to action plans and project deliverables.

Principles

Definition

Having a working definition of Organisational Culture is very important for changing and shaping it. Business leaders need a definition that they can work with. It does not need to be scientifically precise but practical and useable.

We define Organisational Culture as '…a set of shared basic tools, in the form of values, beliefs, behaviours, operating manners and processes, that a group uses to solve its problems.' Our definition is a combination of Schein's and Sorensen's, as it reflects our own management experience.

The word 'shared' plays an important part in the definition. Any individual can possess their personal values, beliefs, or behaviours different from those of the whole, but that does not mean that they can change the culture of the organisation on their own. 'Shared' here signifies a critical mass. One can be tempted to throw in other variables, too, such as philosophies, symbols, norms, rules, traditions, etc.; however, at some level, all these elements can be reduced to values, beliefs, behaviours, operating manners, or processes in one way or another.

Toolkit For Cultural Change

Thus far in the book, we have discussed three foundational elements that must be in place for effective leadership in any company. They are:
- Governing Objective (Maximising Sustainable Owners' Value)
- Vision (Purpose, Values, Behaviours, and Operating Manners)
- Management Model (Value Goals, Risk Appetite, Strategy Development, Decision-Making, and Management Agenda)

Together, we have called these elements the 'Blueprint'. In defining the Blueprint, the company's leadership is crystal clear in how the firm operates – or, in other words, how it 'solves its problems in the form of values, beliefs, behaviours, operating manners, and processes'. Moreover, in very simple terms, the Blueprint gives all colleagues a choice about whether the organisation is right for them. In our experience, it is a critical early step in culture change to encourage colleagues to make that choice.

Actions

We suggest that the 'magic' of Organisational Culture change is to co-create as many of the elements of the Blueprint as possible across the company while explaining (patiently) all the elements. We must stress that it is especially important, where possible and without using it as an excuse to reject change, to respect the heritage of a company or its founders and weave the Blueprint within this context. That said, there will be a point where direction takes the place of co-creation; after all, there are several elements that are non-negotiable.

Once the Blueprint is defined and agreed upon, we recommend that resources are allocated to launch and share it across the firm – if possible, by the co-creators. As per another of our key beliefs ('there are no unimportant people and there are no unimportant jobs'), we recommend that, to the greatest degree possible, no elements are diluted, and everybody's contribution is valued.

Of course, let there be no doubt that the definition and launch of the Blueprint is the easy part – it's just the tip of the iceberg. It's what happens below the surface post-launch that will shape the breadth and depth of culture change. Yet, the Blueprint allows the right seeds to be planted.

Bear in mind that you don't have too many shots at this. Perhaps, if you are a newly appointed CEO, you can do it in the first year of your tenure if you intend to change fundamentally the Strategy of the organisation. Or perhaps you can also do it if there is a big issue the organisation is struggling with that warrants a redefinition of its Vision. By and large, the opportunities to shape fundamentally the culture of the organisation are few and far between. Leaders must be aware of this and use the chance when it presents itself. This would be the moment to turn Organisational Culture into an enabler of delivering the organisational strategy. If that moment is missed, then the existing culture will become an impenetrable barrier.

Finally, over recent assignments, we have become attracted to the discipline of Behavioural Science and would recommend that all companies (to the largest extent possible) build the capabilities to assess, intervene, monitor, and report (comprehensively) on behavioural risk. The new norms can be facilitated more effectively by complementing the Blueprint with colleagues whose role is to observe how it is being put into practice.

Potential Pitfalls

The biggest potential pitfall is attempting to change Behaviours before addressing the shared Values and Behaviours of the organisation. Some leaders like to employ some quite forceful tactics to that effect:

- Using fear (disciplinary threats, punishments, layoffs) as a main tool to change behaviours. It can have quick effects, but it is unsustainable in the long run. If this is your primary modus operandi, your best people will leave, and before you know it, you will be surrounded by 'Yes' people.

- Using money (salaries, bonuses, benefits-in-kind) as the only tool to change behaviours. It is very effective for those who are primarily motivated by money; however, it is also self-defeating in the long run. Firstly, you always run the risk of the best people leaving for more money somewhere else. Second, the people who are likely to stay could turn out to be too self-centred, which is likely to lead to all sorts of other problems (as discussed in Chapter 28).
- Forcing a Blueprint on the organisation at speed without co-creating it with colleagues. As a result, no one in the company will own it as theirs and follow it of their own accord.

12. Operating Rhythm: Why It Is Important and How to Set It

Issue: Everything in a company occurs in cycles, and a failure to manage these cycles with intention leads to diminished efficiency and effectiveness.

Everything in nature operates in cycles; for example, the moon revolves around the earth, the earth revolves around the sun, and the sun revolves around the centre of the galaxy. This causes everything on Earth to operate in cycles – day, night, seasons, etc. As a result, human beings operate in cycles – waking state, sleep state, circadian cycles, breakfast/lunch/dinner, etc. As a matter of fact, people are attracted to cycles and repetition because some element of routine provides certainty and security.

As such, it would be remiss not to recognise and use this universal principle in managing a company. After all, a company is just a collection of people, and it does not make decisions or operate on its own. If you look closely, you can easily see that everything in a company does, and must, happen in recurring cycles that are dependent on each other – from setting the strategy down to informal meetings with close colleagues. We call this 'Operating Rhythm'. We have borrowed this term from Six Sigma, where it is defined as: 'a process of communication between departments to ensure that operations are not interrupted.' Our definition, which we provide in the next section, is broader than that.

The problem with many companies is not that they don't have processes operating in recurring cycles but that these process cycles are not synchronised with each other in a single Operating Rhythm. For example, the financial planning process is not linked to the strategic planning process, the ExCo meeting calendar is not linked to the Board meetings calendar, or the ExCo meetings are not focused on the Management Agenda. The lack of a thoughtfully laid out Operating Rhythm that everyone in a company must follow inevitably leads to:

- Disruption of the best-laid plans
- Inconsistent decision-making
- Surprising results – both wins and failures
- Lack of proper prioritisation of time and resources
- Frequent breakdowns in communication, etc.

In fact, a proper Operating Rhythm is the backbone of everything we have talked about so far, including:

- Purpose
- Values
- Behaviours
- Operating Manners
- Value Goal Setting
- Risk Appetite
- Strategy
- Management Agenda
- Integrated Planning
- Execution
- Decision-Making
- Organisational Design
- Culture

Principles

Definition

Our definition of Operating Rhythm is broader than the Six Sigma one. Namely, it is the set of interdependent cyclical processes as explicitly defined by management in any company. There are two points worth making here.

First, note that the cyclical processes are interdependent. Neither in nature nor in a company can cyclical processes be found that are completely independent. Usually, macrocycles are composed of smaller micro cycles, and they all must be managed appropriately. For example, the yearly financial reporting cycle is composed of nested quarterly and monthly financial reporting cycles.

Second, note that the cyclical processes must be explicitly defined by management. This means that unless the processes in the Operating Rhythm are set by intentional design, they are not part of the Operating Rhythm of the company. There are many processes like these, e.g., having a morning coffee in the office!

The main benefits of designing an Operating Rhythm for your company include:

- Increasing the robustness of the Management Model and its ability to withstand pressure
- Increasing the predictability and stability of the company
- Increasing the dependence on systems while reducing the dependence on individuals

Calendar

Each process of the Operating Rhythm must be defined around a set of recurring dates in the calendar. For example, the monthly ExCo meeting occurs on Thursday of the third week of every month, followed by a monthly Board meeting on the Wednesday of the fourth week of every month. This makes the process more predictable and allows all participants in it to plan their own activities around it. Imagine the chaos if the ExCo meeting or the Board meeting in the above example did not follow a predictable pattern. Of course, it would not be impossible to prepare, but the effort and the resources would be disproportionate.

Synchronisation

All process cycles in the company must be explicitly synchronised and integrated with each other. The daily cycles must be nested within the weekly cycles, which, in turn, must be nested in the monthly cycles and so on, until the long-term cycles are defined. Examples of long-term cycles include setting the company's Value Goals and Vision or the design of the LTIP.

Standardised Agenda

Where meetings are involved as a part of the process cycles, they must be run off a pre-defined, standardised agenda. We have found this to be a particularly useful tool in eliminating unpredictability and boosting the stability of the Operating Rhythm.

Standard Keeper

In any company, many of the cyclical management processes culminate in the office of the CEO. It is the CEO who is ultimately responsible for the proper running of the company on behalf of the owners. Hence, we have found that there is no better standard keeper of the Operating Rhythm than the CEO. The CEO can delegate the Operating Rhythm design and delegate the running of the processes that define it; for example, to the Company Secretary or CSO, but holding people to account must remain their prerogative.

Actions

From The CEO's Perspective

Setting the Operating Rhythm of the company must always begin from the perspective of the CEO, as it is one of their main tools for managing the company. We think a CEO should identify all key important cyclical processes in their company under different time horizons and specifically define them. They should set the macro rhythm first (three-to-five-year cycle), then work their way down, as all processes in the company tie into one big cycle that pulsates annually, monthly, weekly, and daily for each member of staff. We note an example below:

1. Medium-Term (three-to-five years) Cycles:
   - Setting the company Value Goals
   - Resetting the Vision (Purpose, Values, Behaviours, Operating Manners) if needed
   - Refreshing the Management Team (and Board), etc.
2. Annual Cycles
   - Setting the Strategy
   - Testing the Organisational Design versus the Strategy

- Adapting the Management Model to the Strategy
- Reporting the Annual results
- Testing the Risk Appetite Statement
- Integrating and delivering the Strategic and Financial Planning Process
- Defining the Management Agenda and the related Execution Plans
- Setting Objectives and carrying out appraisals
- Managing performance (business and individual), etc.

3. Quarterly Cycles
- Reporting quarterly results
- Communicating progress to key stakeholders, etc.

4. Monthly Cycles
- Board meetings
- ExCo meetings
- Internal communications, etc…

5. Weekly Cycles
- 1:1 meeting with direct reports
- 1:1 meeting with Board members, etc…

The above is by no means an exhaustive list of all the crucial cyclical processes. It all depends on the company and the industry it operates in. The key is to identify what these processes are and intentionally synchronise them.

From an Individual Perspective

Every individual should also make an effort to synchronise their own working schedules and routines with the broader company Operating Rhythm. Depending on the department that they are working in, their job might include direct involvement in many of the above processes. Understanding the interdependence of the processes and their cyclicality will allow for better execution of one's own job. On a personal level, a very simple example is to synchronise your own one-to-one meeting with your boss just before or just after their one-to-one meeting with their boss. This will allow for timely communication and delegation.

Potential Pitfalls

Rigidity

Becoming too rigid about the Operating Rhythm could become an issue when it is applied without the flexibility of thought or action. There are always going to be unforeseen circumstances and out-of-cycle issues that must be dealt with, e.g., unexpected competitive moves or M&A opportunities. Dealing with such issues should be allowed within the cyclical processes. For instance, there must be a way to avail of out-of-cycle investment opportunities when they present themselves instead of waiting for the next year's planning cycle. Another example is to keep a place on the standardised meeting agenda for matters not covered elsewhere. The Operating Rhythm is supposed to liberate more time for thinking and action rather than making the company inflexible and rigid.

Gaming

Some managers may attempt to game the Operating Rhythm by pushing through their pet projects as out-of-cycle issues, thereby seeking precedence over the opportunities and issues being managed through the cycle and the Management Agenda. The CEO should be mindful of such possibilities and deal with them as any other attempt at gaming: through the application of the principles of good decision-making, making the distinction between short-term targets and long-term Value Goals and the maintaining the integrity of the Management Agenda.

Cycle Disruption

It is always very tempting to allow the next crisis to jump to the top of the attention queue with no prioritisation or trade-off mechanism. This temptation should be resisted as much as possible.

13. Corporate Communications: How to Communicate Effectively

Issue: Nothing gets done in a company without communication, yet many people do not know how to communicate effectively with each other.

Communication at work takes place in various ways: face-to-face conversations, emails, messages, phone calls, presentations, memos, etc. Corporate citizens use a variety of tools to communicate: Zoom, Outlook, PowerPoint, Word, Slack, GoToMeeting, and Skype, as well as hundreds of specialised tools for task management, workflow or resource management, whiteboard collaboration, or brainstorming. Of course, good communication skills are at the heart of everything in corporate life, and yet while the communication tools do help, sometimes they only mask an underlying issue or challenge.

Many people misunderstand what good communication is. Some think that good communication is supplying a lot of information. You will find their emails, memos, or presentations densely packed with context, facts, or everything they think is relevant. Others think that any information outside a very narrow focus is bad, so their communications are sparse and short, making you wonder if they have missed something important. Some think that fancy formatting is crucial to good communication, while others think fancy formatting distracts from the message. Some strive to use sophisticated language, while others aim for the simplest language possible. All the above could be either right or wrong, but what is certain is that the core principles of good communication are not wholly dependent on such issues.

Messy written or verbal communication often means messy thinking. In our careers, we have used a simple test: if you can't write it down or say it clearly, you haven't thought about it well enough. Unfortunately, communicating is more often learnt on the job than at school or university. This means a lot of trial and error.

For example, if the communication with your own team is ineffective, you won't be able to achieve your objectives, and if the communication with your boss is ineffective, then you will not help them make the right decisions. Poor communication skills can kill even the best strategy, leaving people unsure of where they stand, or what tasks they need to perform.

Principles

We would like to share some practical ideas and tools that will help you help you immediately, without speaking at length about topics like who your audience is or what your message is. There are many excellent books about how to communicate effectively that you can read in your own time if you want to pursue this further.[9]

1. Start with transparent communication. With your team, start from the premise of 'share everything and work your way backwards' rather than 'share nothing and work your way forwards'. A collaborative culture is based on full disclosure, trust, and integrity – having the courage to stand up and share on an adult-to-adult basis. Of course, there are natural constraints (such as market abuse rules) and thinking about messaging and timing is critical, but the key point of principle is 'full information sharing all of the time', thereby treating your team as adults.

2. Share information in an undiluted way. One of the great fallacies of corporate life is that colleagues are less interested in, or are unable to understand, the strategy of the business or progress against delivery promises. In our experience, most colleagues do have a 'connection' with the company and are genuinely interested in what's happening. So, share the messages in an

---

[9] We recommend *The Pyramid Principle* by Barbara Minto.

undiluted way, spend time explaining the intricacies (in particular, at annual or half-year results time) and encourage questions.

3. Share information with everyone. There are no unimportant people, and no unimportant jobs, etc with everyone having the right to be informed, regardless of title, job role, or place in the hierarchy.

4. Effective communication has a purpose. Communicating or sharing information for its own sake is a waste of time and resources if nobody's interested in what you have to say. Below are some simple rules for communicating in a way to help you achieve your aspirations (we recognise the list below might be perceived as 'motherhood and apple pie' by many readers, but for the sake of completeness, we include them here):

- Intention: There must always be a clear purpose (or intention) for communicating (the 'why'). Communicating without 'the why' does not make any sense. Moreover, you should always let the other party know why you are sending them an email or presenting to them if it is not obvious from the context. Copying people on emails without letting them know why is a bad practice.

- Action/Decision: Good communication should always lead to a decision or an action (the 'so what'). You must also let the other party know what you want from them and what action or decision is expected from them. If there is none, you would be better off withholding the communication. It is also acceptable to tell them that what you are giving them is for information purposes only, as well as in what context this information might be useful. It is then up to the recipient as to whether they read the information. Finally, it is always a good practice to accompany the 'so what' with a deadline, which is when you'd expect them to take the action or the decision.

- Argument: If the 'so what' is not obvious to the other party, then good communication always includes a logical argument (or a logical story) about how to arrive at it. This story or argument should be easy to follow. Most of the time, it is useful to outline the underlying principles behind the story or argument before delving deep into the facts – this helps the recipient orientate themselves as to your direction of thinking.

103

This is where neat formatting can be handy in the case of written communication, as it allows the reader to follow your story or argument more readily. In addition, if there are some obvious counterarguments that could come to mind, you should explicitly include them in this section. Finally, note that the 'so what' precedes the argument, even though most people's natural tendency is to build an argument before presenting the conclusion. The reason for this is to save time for the decision-maker or action-taker, which is very important in the context of business.

5. Effective communication is timely. It is always a good practice to respond quickly without delay. If you need time to formulate your response, you should still acknowledge the receipt of the information quickly by saying how much time you need to prepare your proper response and/or renegotiate the deadline – never ever carry ambiguity about the 'when'. If you are on the receiving end of a messy communication, do not be afraid to ask for clarification.

6. Your audience matters. Good communication should always be tailored specifically to the other side, and this includes the formality, context, language, and length of the argument. For example, if you are a middle manager, it might be inappropriate to send a text message or even an email to the members of the Board of Directors, whereas sending them a well-thought-through and structured presentation might be better suited to their expectations. It is a good idea to use your common sense here, and if you are unsure about it, then you should consult your boss.

7. Effective communication does not depend on the medium. The principles above do not depend on the medium of communication, whether it is PowerPoint, Word, email, instant message or else, although choosing the right medium might increase your chances of conveying your message clearly.

Actions

Communication Standards

We have found that establishing standards or rules for effective communications can help tremendously the overall effectiveness of any organisation. In our experience, the areas best suited for standardisation are email communications and presentations to ExCo, the Board of Directors, and their sub-committees. Standardising email communications can lead to a jump in productivity accompanied by a huge reduction in the number of emails circulating in the organisation. Standardising presentation templates for senior committees and sub-committees helps increase the quality and the speed of decision-making. There could also be communication standards for internal (staff, senior management) and external (investors, regulators) communications.

Standard Keepers

Effective communication standards will be quickly forgotten without standard keepers. For example, the standard keeper for senior committees' presentations could be the Company Secretary or, in certain cases pertaining to the Vision, Strategy, and IPP, the CSO. Both the Company Secretary and the CSO could also act as gatekeepers if standards are not met.

Training

Regardless of your level in the organisation, it is important to train both yourself and your team to communicate effectively. This is not something to be underestimated or delayed.

Potential Pitfalls

Blaming the medium of communication for the inefficiency of communication is the single biggest pitfall. For example, PowerPoint has been widely blamed for poor communication – it is called 'death by PowerPoint'. We think that this is unfair. PowerPoint, and indeed any other presentation or editing software, is only as good at communication as its user.

We have all heard the story of Jeff Bezos banning PowerPoint at Amazon in 2004, swapping it for two-to-six-page memos. In the original email explaining the decision Bezos said: 'The reason writing a good four-page memo is harder than 'writing' a twenty-page PowerPoint is because the narrative structure of a good memo forces better thought and a better understanding of what's more important than what and how things are related. PowerPoint-style presentations somehow give permission to gloss over ideas, flatten out any sense of relative importance, and ignore the interconnectedness of ideas.'[10] Clearly Bezos was frustrated by the communications of colleagues and decided to change this by altering the medium. Undoubtedly, Bezos thought that re-training people on how to write effective arguments in PowerPoint was going to be more costly and time-consuming than taking them suddenly and completely out of their comfort zone by banning PowerPoint altogether.

In any event, the underlying principle here is not the 'medium' per se but the quality of the communication – we return to where we started, namely: 'if you can't write it down or say it clearly, you haven't thought about it well enough'. As with every dimension of this book, good thinking is the pre-requisite for good doing.

---

[10] Ram Charan and Julia Yang, *The Amazon Management System: The Ultimate Digital Business Engine That Creates Extraordinary Value for Both Customers and Shareholders*, Idea Press Publishing, 2019.

14. Meetings: How to Conduct Meetings Effectively

Issue: A lot of time is wasted in ineffective meetings in the corporate world, but it does not have to be this way.

Meetings have become a huge time waster in many companies around the world. So much so that the term 'meeting madness' has gained popularity in business circles. One can find numerous academic studies of how ineffective meetings pervade at most companies. It is both a ridiculous and a fascinating story of the modern age.

The issue is compounded by the fact that other people can now access your electronic calendar remotely for availability. Even if you have a personal assistant who manages your diary, they might not be able to protect you from being invited to a lot of time-wasting meetings.

It does not matter if the meeting is in person or over Zoom. It can be ineffective for several reasons, such as:

- People don't know why they have been invited, or they don't even have to be there in the first place.
- Meetings are way too long, e.g., what can be done in five minutes can take up hours to discuss.
- Some people use meetings to justify their own need to be constantly busy or to exert control over others – both of which are stress-coping strategies discussed in Chapter 27.
- Dialogue participation is uneven – some people dominate the airwaves, while others don't speak at all.

- Some people do not pay due attention, e.g., they are sending text messages or emails while in the meeting.

Poor meetings lead to undesirable results, such as:

- Wasted time, which is the only truly scarce resource in any company
- Morale deterioration
- Increased staff turnover

If you look closely at how meetings are conducted in any one company, you can usually guess relatively well how effective or ineffective its Management Model is and whether the principles of Management Agenda and effective decision-making are being applied as they should. Ironically, meeting effectiveness is also a good indicator of expected performance.

For example, one of the authors (Emil) once experienced a meeting crisis while working in the banking sector. There were weeks when Emil spent forty hours in meetings alone, which was clearly an unsustainable schedule, leading to many issues. He experimented with different solutions until choosing to make Wednesdays meeting-free and blocked enough time in the calendar during the other weekdays that could not be usurped by meetings.

The other author (Jeremy) found it impossible, pre-inception of the Management Agenda, to maintain adequate time for thinking and reading as a critical element of managing oneself (see Section 4).

There have been attempts in some companies to ban meetings altogether, but this is not a sustainable and effective solution. After all, meetings are essential for collaboration and innovation in the workplace. If you are like us, you will need others around you to bounce ideas off, discuss strategies, and, in general, be creative.

Principles

The personal time of everyone involved in a meeting is extremely valuable. It must be respected and preserved by applying the following principles:

Purpose and Agenda

Every meeting must have both. Having a purpose means being clear in the invitation to the meeting about what is going to be accomplished – for example, decide, get a briefing, have a brainstorm, etc. Having an agenda means being clear in the invitation about how you are going to accomplish your purpose – for example, by presentation, discussion, vote, etc.

Failure to specify both a purpose and an agenda of the meeting will result in an irreversible waste of time for all attendees.

Attendees

Everyone on the invitee list must know why they are there by reviewing the agenda and the purpose of the meeting. Those who are unclear on why they have been invited should be free to reject attendance.

There are three types of attendees:

- Chair. This is usually the one who calls the meeting, but not always. At Board meetings, it would be the Chairman, whereas at ExCo meetings, it would be the CEO. For a one-to-one meeting with your boss, it should be you. The Chair ensures that the agenda is followed, and the purpose is accomplished within the allocated time. The Chair also invites people to speak and vote. They are always aiming to move the conversation forwards (see Effective Participation Principle below).
- Participants. Usually, these are the individuals with decision rights on the issue or the members of a collective organisational body, such as the ExCo or the Board.
- Specialists. Certain official meetings might have their own designated minute-takers or timekeepers, such as the official Company Secretary.

Time

Time is the most valuable resource for everyone at the meeting. Starting and finishing on time treats everyone with respect. When unsure how much time to allocate for a meeting, err on the side of less.

As a rule of thumb, one-to-one meetings should not take more than thirty minutes; routine meetings as part of the Operating Rhythm (see below) should not take more than an hour, while Board and ExCo meetings should not take more than four hours (with exceptions depending on the issues at hand).

It's also good practice to schedule meetings that allow participants time to take a break between the end of the meeting and the next commitment (whether that be another meeting or call). There's nothing worse than back-to-back commitments without a 'firebreak'.

Operating Rhythm Synchronisation

The aspiration should be that all meetings are individual parts of the company's Operating Rhythm. The only exceptions should be driven by unpredictable events. This means that most of the meetings must be scheduled well in advance. Also, when a meeting is a routine part of the Operating Rhythm, its agenda and purpose must be standardised and should not change too often. This will give all participants a chance to prepare thoroughly in advance.

Preparation

Distribution of materials for pre-read is the absolute best practice, and enough time must be given to participants to prepare. Not reading the pre-read materials disrespects everyone's time. It's up to the Chair of the meeting to decide how to proceed if someone is not ready.

Sometimes it is worth meeting attendees individually in advance of an important meeting to address their concerns if the stakes are high or the time to make the decision is short.

Effective Participation

The first key to effective participation is to aim to move the conversation forward in line with the objective of the meeting. This means strictly not going back to previous points if the conversation has already moved forward. This requires speaking on time at the right moment, not later. One must always be asking oneself, 'Is what I am going to say going to move the conversation forward?'. As we pointed out above, this is also one of the Chair's main responsibilities.

The second key to effective participation is to give one's full undivided attention to whatever is going on in the meeting at any moment. This means no playing with electronic devices unless for taking notes.

Follow Up

Minutes, decisions, and/or action points must always be distributed after the meeting via the Chair or the meeting secretariat.

The CEO can choose to codify the above principles as 'Meetings Ground Rules' as a part of the Operating Manners discussed in Chapter 2.

Actions

There are a number of actions that could be considered:

1. The Chair of a meeting must ensure that:

- The Purpose and the Agenda are distributed in advance.
- Only required participants are invited, and attendance of critical participants is confirmed in advance (a meeting with a too-large participant list is always a warning sign).
- The meeting begins and ends on time.
- Everyone in the meeting is invited to participate and share their point of view. To accomplish this, the Chair should not: (i) allow any participant to highjack the conversation completely; and (ii) allow any participant to hide or be intimidated into silence by others and should clearly encourage the 'quiet ones' to contribute.
- The conversation is always moving forward (see above).
- The meeting has breaks to allow participants to focus and regain energy.
- Minutes, decisions, and action points are recorded and distributed at the end, and there is no ambiguity as to 'Who/ What/ When/ Why'.
- They exhibit the right behaviours; in our experience, this includes setting the mood and tempo; knowing when to bring in each skillset or opinion; showing authority without dominating the meeting; being restrained; being patient but focused; showing good awareness of team dynamics; and withholding their own views until all have spoken.
- (If the meeting is physical) they sit in the right place around the executive table; what we find works best is for the Chair to sit in the

middle of the table and not at the head (sitting at the head feels like a power play to participants).

2. Invited attendees should:

- Feel free to refuse to attend meetings without a purpose and an agenda.
- Clarify with the Chair why they have been invited if it is unclear.
- Study the pre-read materials in advance.
- Arrive on time.
- Give their full attention, i.e., no use of electronic devices except for notetaking.
- Participate in a timely manner so as to always take the conversation towards accomplishing the purpose of the meeting.
- Read and execute, if required, the follow-up minutes, decisions, and/or action points before the next meeting of the same operating cycle.

3. Finally, we would like to make a few points about one-to-one meetings. This critical element of the Operating Rhythm should be owned by the 'Colleague' and not by the 'Boss'. This is a chance to talk about non-Management Agenda items as prompted by the 'Colleague', and we suggest focusing on building a psychologically safe environment for feedback (see Radical Candor™ in Chapter 22).

That said, we think that the 'Colleague' must prepare a written one-to-one form in advance of every session, and the 'Boss' should use the form and the conversation to satisfy themselves that the line of business or function is being led to the highest standards of the Management Model. Indeed, in our experience, 'A-players' (as defined in Chapter 19) use the one-to-one as a stage to demonstrate competence and the confidence to debate real issues at hand (including areas of personal development) – the one-to-one will not work if it turns into a sales pitch (which can occur). The one-to-one is another useful insight into a colleague's ability to provide a balanced view of themselves – assuming the culture allows for such transparency.

In our experience, the worst one-to-one meetings are those in which there is not agenda, no pre-read, no issues for debate, and no feedback conversations. A notebook with a few notes, a one-way conversation, a list of housekeeping items, a lack of spark, and a closed mind are all tell-tale signs of a sub-optimal relationship between 'Boss' and 'Colleague' that will never grow either party.

Potential Pitfalls

First, if others don't follow these principles, you should speak up. Talk to your boss and get them on your side. Nobody wants to waste valuable resources, and that includes time. Also, in your own sphere of influence, run your meetings properly. Set an example.

Second, what if your boss is negligent with meetings and is a time waster? It might sound bizarre, but this is very common in the corporate world. There are many managers and executives who don't value their own time and the time of others. There are also many others who enjoy hijacking meetings to display control and self-importance. The good news is that you are not completely helpless in this situation. You can try and convince your boss that it is their valuable time that is being wasted, and at the same time, you can set an example as to how meetings can be run effectively when you are the Chair.

15. Consultants: When to Use or Not

Issue: Many companies become over-dependent on external consultants to the extent that their own ability to formulate strategy and execute it suffers.

Hiring consultants has an important place in business; however, many companies use this resource in the wrong way. It's tempting to use consultants if your company can afford it. In the short run, it brings about instant gratification in terms of results, much like eating a big meal gives rise to instant gratification in terms of pleasure. Yet, if you do this consistently over the long run, then it is likely to catch up with you.

Using consultants too much can erode in-house skills, alienate the workforce, and restrict the inability to react quickly on your own – not to mention the huge bill at the end of each month. Of course, there are industries, such as private equity, which rely on consultants and advisers as a part of their day-to-day business model. We are not talking about them here.

Companies that indulge in using consultants rarely stick to just one firm or individual. Such companies engage many and various consultants at every level of the organisation.

When the total bill finally catches up, and these companies decide to get rid of the consultants they hired, it usually transpires that they can no longer carry out some critical tasks on their own without external help. The use of consultants has produced what is sometimes called a 'shadow workforce'.

This is not the only issue. The use of consultants is one of the ways companies can adopt best practices. However, this has a flipside, as, after some point, there is a risk that all companies adopt the same best practice and innovation is stifled. Thus, extensive use of consultants can lead to mediocrity and dependence across entire industries over the long term. Many companies have fallen into this trap over time.

Principles

To avoid overreliance on consultants and the creation of a shadow workforce, we suggest the following tests when deciding to hire or terminate the contract of a specific consultant:

1. Need Test: Is there a specific skill/expertise gap that we cannot fill internally or through recruitment in the time available? This is the most important question and should be answered first. Clearly, if there is a gap in capability, it is acceptable to turn to external help.

2. Time Test: Even if we can fill that gap, is there a time-critical element to it? There is also the possibility that the capability exists but that it cannot be mobilised as quickly as it should. If this is the case, the hiring of consultants is also justified.

3. Productivity Test: Do we need a productivity boost in a specific area of our business? There is the possibility that we do have the capability, but our capacity is inadequate for the time we must complete the specific job. In this case, hiring eternal help through interims or contractors is also justified as a boost to productivity.

4. Objectivity Test: Do we need an external (more objective) view on any area of our business? Sometimes we would have both the time and the capacity, but we need an outside view on a specific issue or area of the business that we cannot provide internally because of too much vested interest or conflicts of interest. In this case, bringing in external help without any preconceived ideas about the issue could be beneficial.

We would like to illustrate this with an example from our own experience. We used to work for a bank which suffered significantly during the 2008 financial crisis. When we joined the bank, it was critically ill – morale was at an all-time low, people working there were tired and scared for their jobs, and there were many skill and expertise gaps. On top of that, there were several pressing issues from the market, owners, and Regulators that could not wait to be managed.

The only way to address the above issues effectively and at pace was to hire external consultants. It was expensive relative to hiring our own experts, but it was the only way. There was a need, time was of critical importance, and some of the questions required an unbiased and objective view that only an external adviser could bring. At the same time, we started a hiring process with the idea of bridging the skills/expertise gap as soon as possible.

It took us almost two years before we were able to bring in-house the activities in many of the functional areas that we were delegating. This, however, came at a cost, which was significantly higher than doing it alone – although this was not an option given the circumstances. Towards the end of this transitional period, we also insisted that there was a formal transfer of skills before the consultants left the business.

Yet, there was one functional area – the Risk Function – where we failed our own tests. It was much more difficult to hire people with risk management expertise at that time, and the regulatory demands were continuously becoming more stringent and onerous. For these reasons, we allowed the consultants to continue much longer than in other areas of the bank. As a result, many different consultants (both day-rate individuals and companies) were hired while the bank struggled to hire and build its own expertise, which led to the creation of a shadow workforce. The problem gradually became endemic. We should have managed it differently and better by asking the questions above and then, importantly, avoided the pitfalls detailed at the end of this chapter.

Actions

There are a number of actions that could be considered:

1. When hiring consultants, make sure that it is with a specific goal, which, all things being equal, is explicitly linked to the Management Agenda. Even when all the tests above are met, if bringing in consultants cannot be linked to the Management Agenda, then it should not be important enough to dedicate resources – any exceptions should be subject to rigorous challenge and debate.

In addition, the goal should always be linked to a specific timeframe, as good project management practices dictate.

Most consultants are very skilled at 'time extension' or 'scope creep' (that's a compliment), so it is incumbent on management to be extremely disciplined with the allocation of the company's resources to the highest-value issues and opportunities – if it's not on the Management Agenda (and even if you're frustrated with performance or capability) then the allocation of resources to consultants should be avoided and 'performance management' the focus.

2. Ensure that the consultants' skills and expertise required for the assignment are transferred in-house, thereby reducing future dependency on consultants. We always insist consultants train our own people in the capabilities that are required to do the job. If the consultants are not willing or incapable of doing this, we will always look elsewhere.

3. Consider centralising the procurement and management of consultants under the CTO (a role discussed earlier) to avoid the creation of a shadow workforce. Such centralisation is not always possible and would depend on the size and the Organisational Design of your company; however, if possible, it should be considered as best practice.

Potential Pitfalls

There are a number of pitfalls that one must be aware of:

1. Avoid hiring consultants 'in haste'. No matter the time pressure, build a factbase, look at alternative suppliers, and take references – good procurement practices are essential.

2. Avoid 'time extension' or 'scope creep'. Stick to the brief where any new work also goes through the questions detailed above; at minimum, use the techniques of the Management Agenda.

3. Avoid 'consultant as comfort blanket'. Do not abdicate from 'performance management' responsibilities by adding a layer between you and your team. There's something wrong with the team if this is the case – 'if you can't change the people, change the people'.

4. Avoid 'marginal gain disease'. There will be a point in time when the best course of action is to let your own people take the reins; a balanced judgement is when the risk of imperfection is more than compensated for by the cost saving and the trust shared with colleagues.

5. Avoid 'cost surprises'. Always ensure that the consultants' fee parameters are agreed upon before any piece of work commences – irrespective of how small.

6. Avoid the 'hourly rate' relationship if possible. This can add up to a significant cost if not careful. It is not unknown for companies to employ such consultants for years. Good management information on how consultants are utilised is important to avoid lingering and long-term consulting costs.

7. Avoid 'poor knowledge transfer'. Agree in advance the specific and granular tools and tests that will be used to embed knowledge transfer – you cannot afford to have the consultants return to the same gig time after time.

SECTION 3 – MANAGING ONESELF

It is our experience that to be a successful senior leader and CEO, one must be steadfast in setting a Governing Objective on the one hand, and on the other, bring this to life through an emotionally attractive Vision and a rational Management Model that enable colleagues to be the very best they can be. However, and this is a big 'however', a key requirement for the effectiveness of any leader is the ability to manage oneself.

Managing oneself is not traditionally taught in MBA programmes around the world. In studying management science, there is a strong focus on how to manage and motivate others but little or no time is spent on the critical domain of 'managing oneself'. The assumption is that it is the same – it is not.

Even the most intelligent leaders and CEOs can sabotage their best intentions through messy organisation of themselves.

The presence of a Governing Objective, Vision, and Management Model is insufficient to deliver great results if the leader cannot set priorities and allocate time effectively. In many ways, the leader's actions will lack integrity as they will not be aligned with the firm's Values and Behaviours. For example, a fact-based, alternatives-driven approach to decision-making underpinned by strategy development and a Governing Objective may not align with the leader's own day-to-day behaviours and actions, which will inevitably both confuse and call into question the integrity of the Blueprint.

One dictionary definition of being a manager is 'a person responsible for supervising and motivating employees and for directing the progress of an organisation.' In other words, the manager is expected 'to get a job done through others'. Now, how can one manage, let alone motivate, even one other person if one cannot manage oneself? Imagine being responsible for thousands of employees, even hundreds of thousands. Consider the missed opportunity if one can't manage oneself.

Leading Without Winging It

We have known and worked for many C-Suite executives who were terrible at managing themselves. We often wondered how they became senior leaders in the first place. This is just more evidence that when big corporations promote from within, they are not necessarily interested in their candidates' ability to manage themselves. As a matter of fact, the complex and complicated Organisational Structures of such companies often provide a safety net for people who are bad at self-management.

Unfortunately, both the individual and the company can pay a high cost where poor self-management practices lead to confusion and misunderstanding. At an organisation level, colleagues try and imitate such behaviours thinking wrongly that managing in this way is the reason why such leaders have been so 'successful'. At an individual level, failure to manage oneself effectively means that 'optimised outcomes' will never be delivered (and, likely, will impact on health and well-being in the long term).

What we mean by 'managing oneself' is simple: knowing what to commit to and how to keep those commitments in the most effective and efficient manner, i.e.:

- Setting the right personal priorities (Chapter 16)
- Managing your time to these priorities (Chapter 17)
- Avoiding exhausting yourself in the process (Chapter 18)

Note that nothing in this definition points to how to interact, manage, or motivate other people. We reiterate that unless you know how to set your own priorities and manage your time effectively, you cannot manage anyone else effectively either. Let's now investigate these elements in more detail.

16. Priorities Management: How to Set the Right Personal Priorities

*Issue: **The inability to identify correctly your own personal priorities can jeopardise the priorities of the organisation.***

Managing oneself is not about running an organisation and the people that work in it. It is not about setting the company Vision and Strategy, or their Execution. It is not about motivating and leading others to do what you have asked them to. Instead, it is about how you manage and conduct yourself in a relationship with others and your own time.

Many people managers, including senior executives, do not understand this when they first hear it. Most of them appreciate why it is important to manage and lead others, and yet they lack the right disciplines to manage themselves correctly, including setting their own personal priorities.

If you look back at your career you will discover that you have most certainly once worked for someone who created chaos and sabotaged the best intentions of the people around them. This is often driven by deep-seated, sub-conscious impulses such as being seen to be busy, attention-seeking, fear, the need for domination over others, etc. It was as if their priority was to satisfy those impulses rather than lead their people in the right direction. In other words, their own personal priorities were in invisible conflict with those of the organisation. That is why attempting to manage others without knowing how to manage oneself is a contradiction with costly side-effects.

Let's illustrate this with three archetypal examples. The first example is a senior executive whose number one priority is the unspoken need to dominate everyone with power and fear. This person is known to fire people if not liking something about them. As a result, the people are scared, which brings about all sorts of negative consequences. Clearly, this senior executive's priorities do not match those of the organisation.

The second example is a senior executive whose number one priority is the unspoken need to be the source of every good idea and action. This person needs to feel more intelligent and more knowledgeable than everyone. This person perceives smart people as a threat. Again, their unrecognised priorities contradict those of the organisation.

The third example is a senior executive whose number one priority is the unspoken need to be the centre of attention. This person needs to feel the respect, adoration, and attention of everyone employing a few tactics to get attention, e.g., being late for meetings and making everyone wait or being intentionally confrontational in meetings to attract attention to himself. Obviously, smart people with healthy self-esteem will not stay long in such an environment.

The common denominator in all examples is that what was most important to these people on a personal level did not match with what was most important for the organisation.

Principles

There are a number of principles that must be applied:

1. The first principle for any senior executive is to remember always that unless they own the organisation they work for, they are an agent of the owners. They find themselves in a position of power to serve the organisation and its owners, not to serve themselves. This mindset links directly to the Governing Objective and is in direct opposition to the mindset of a self-serving individual. Unfortunately, many managers easily and conveniently forget this as they climb the company hierarchy and taste power's sweet flavour.

2. The second principle is just as important as the first. As a senior executive you must aim for alignment along two key dimensions:

- Your words, actions, and behaviours must be aligned with who you are as a person, such as your own personal Values and Principles.

- Your words, actions, and behaviours must be also aligned with the company's Governing Objective, Vision, and Management Model.

We call this alignment 'integrity'. It takes effort and intention to sustain, while lacking thereof is so much easier. If you lack integrity, the people working for you will know this immediately and it will give them a licence to withhold their own integrity and take the easy way out. After all, how can you expect integrity from others if you lack it yourself?

3. The third principle is to stay focused on something bigger than maximising your own self-importance. The Governing Objective, the Vision, and the Management Model are the natural places to focus. It must be obvious to your colleagues that your aspiration as a leader is not to benefit primarily yourself; rather, you are there to benefit them, the organisation, and ultimately, the owners. After all, if the organisation is successful, then everyone, including you, will be successful too. A clearly defined Blueprint that includes the elements defined above is a great way to articulate the 'standards' by which you will be held accountable.

4. Finally, you must acknowledge the costs that your organisation will inevitably pay if you are self-serving and lacking integrity. The list of costs is very long, but most importantly it includes things like creating an environment of mediocrity and wasting valuable resources.

Actions

Leading with integrity requires four things:

1. Communicating to your team and colleagues the Governing Objective, the Vision, and the Management Model and being clear what your and their contribution should be and why you both are creating a common cause and approach. Most importantly, you are clear that is not just a set of rules and procedures to be obeyed but a means to create competitive advantage through having a growth mindset. The objective is to align all – including yourself – with the organisational priorities. The process of objective-setting and performance management will be very helpful here. Chapter 22 is dedicated to this topic.

2. Selecting and recruiting those who will buy into the Blueprint. Of course, selection and recruitment are not fool proof, so it is equally important to manage the performance of those who actively or silently pursue an alternative agenda. In extremis, the CEO must have the courage to let go those who do not fit, irrespective of competence. A regret of one of the authors (Jeremy) was spending too much time trying to persuade colleagues of the veracity of the Blueprint when it was clear there was irreconcilable misalignment.

3. Being a role model. Anything that you want your colleagues to be or do, you must first demonstrate through your own actions and behaviours (consistent with the Blueprint). Unless you do this, people will be very quick to spot even the smallest inconsistency in your behaviour, and they will either imitate you or lose their trust in you.

4. Making good decision-making a core competence. Decisions must be based on transparent principles, which are not influenced by self-importance and personal whim. For example, large M&A transactions are often pursued for the sake of enhancing self-importance, rather than adhering to value-maximisation principles (or 'scale for scale's sake'). Your colleagues and investors need to know how you make decisions and allocate resources (as discussed in an earlier chapter).

Potential Pitfalls

What do you do when some of the people around you lack integrity, maybe even including your own boss? After all, some people just cannot help themselves when they have power and influence. We cannot tell you what to do as it will depend on the particulars of the situation; however, we can tell you to maintain your integrity in each case. This way you can always react appropriately, irrespective of what happens.

17. Time Management: How to Manage Your Time Effectively

Issue: Failure to manage your time smartly will result in waste – period.

Broadly speaking there are four types of resources in a company, which leadership must put to best possible use:

- Financial – the available funds for investment and working capital
- Human – the available personnel working for the company
- IT or Operational Capacity – the available capacity to produce goods or services
- Management Time – the time available at management level to get things done

Even though financial resources can sometimes appear constrained in the short run, in the long run, a company can always raise more capital at a certain price provided that the expected value exceeds that cost of that capital. In this sense, financial resources are never constrained in the long run.

Human resources are very similar. Even if a company has skill gaps and open positions at any point in time, it can always hire or train up more people, given enough time. In addition, it can always throw financial resources at the issue by plugging the short-term gaps with interims or consultants.

IT or Operational Capacity may also look constrained in the short-term, but this issue can always be overcome over time. Even if a company runs on sluggish legacy systems or outdated operational methods, in time it can add to capacity and capability. One should recognise, of course, that in the interim, the prioritisation of, for example, development resource will be a source of much debate, where Decision Rules and Management Agenda are invaluable tools as discussed in earlier chapters.

Management time and one's own personal time as a CEO or senior executive is the only permanently constrained resource. No matter how hard you work, you only get a fixed number of hours in the day. You cannot clone yourself or hire another person to share your tasks. The problem gets harder as you climb up the company hierarchy; the higher up the ladder you go, the smarter you need to be with your own time.

There is a very subtle point to be made here. Time itself is not the real limiting factor, although we do use it as a proxy. Rather, the limiting factor is what you give sufficient attention to in that time. No matter how many people or advisers work for you, you can only give sufficient attention to a limited number of issues in a particular timespan. It is therefore clear that if you are a decision-maker then your capacity to give attention to issues and make decisions is permanently limited.

For example, at a certain stage of our careers we have all experienced the young managers' predicament. Young managers are often tempted to stay in their comfort zone and do the job of their team members just because they know how to do it more efficiently instead of delegating. As a result, they end up working more hours than necessary and are spread so thinly over the time available that they end up overworked and burnt out.

Senior managers are not immune from problems like this. Some often micro-manage their teams because they have a deep-seated need to be in total control and are fearful of letting go. Or managers sometimes want to show off how capable or knowledgeable they are. Unfortunately, the result is the same. In both cases, the managers' productivity takes a significant hit, despite working more hours. This can also lead to various interpersonal conflicts between them and their team members.

Another example we have seen many times is the manager who is both late for meetings and overruns the scheduled time. Their justification is claiming that they really want to go deep into the subject matter of each meeting. While there is nothing wrong with this desire, they are often unprepared (e.g., have not read the advance materials) and do not value the time of the people around them, because they perceive themselves as more important. As a result, people working with them begin undervaluing their own time as well, which only exacerbates the problem. Thus, said manager turns into a constraint to getting things done, instead of being a facilitator of quick decision-making and action.

Finally, we would like to share a story from our management experience. In a company we used to work for we decided to organise a time management seminar for all senior managers and executives. The mistake we made was that we announced the seminar as voluntary attendance, wrongly thinking that people will recognise the need and attend to learn some new skills. What happened was that people who most needed these skills did not attend because they could not find the time. The irony in this case was expensive for the company.

Principles

Hundreds of books have been written about effective time management, yet the principles are simple and straightforward:

1. Focus on the highest-value issues and opportunities. Prioritising time should be directly linked to intrinsic company value. That's why having a Management Agenda is an extremely valuable management tool. It helps everyone from the CEO to all others in the company prioritise what they spend their time on. In addition, for avoidance of any doubt, every people manager from the CEO down must clarify the priorities for each of their direct reports. Thus, everyone in the company will know what is important and what to focus on.

2. Have the courage and discipline to say 'no'. The reality of life is that there will always be new tasks coming in from all directions that are going to claim your attention and time. Unless those tasks fall under the priorities on your Management Agenda, you must either have the courage and discipline to say 'no' or apply the rule of substitution (not incrementalism). Some of the most difficult tasks to say 'no' to will be those coming directly from your boss. Although it is their duty to respect your time (see the next principle), it is not their responsibility to manage it. That is why, if you cannot decide on what is

most important at any moment, you must have a prioritisation discussion with your boss. The same applies when you are delegating a task to the people who work for you – you must never leave them in any doubt as to where and how what you're asking them to do relates to the Management Agenda.

3. Value not only your own time but also the time of the people you work with. Many managers tend to disrespect the time of the people they manage. Who can blame them, given that their own bosses also disrespect their time? We both used to work for people who had the tendency to wreck our carefully planned days completely due to their own inability to organise themselves. We even planned for unplanned boss interventions on a weekly basis. This does not need to be the case if everyone respects not only their own time but also the time of their colleagues. When this is the case, people will come to meetings both prepared and on time.

Actions

There are a number of actions that could be considered:

1. Use the company's Management Agenda, Financial Plan, and your own Performance Contract with your manager to determine the highest-value issues and opportunities at the level of the organisation that you must focus on.

2. If you're the CEO, then you should focus your attention and time exclusively on the Management Agenda. Business as usual (BAU) should be completely delegated and you should intervene only if something is off-track or there is a request for help. Use one-to-one meetings for this.

3. Be as clear as possible about the things that won't get done and communicate them clearly to your boss and team members.

4. Work with the people who report to you to determine the set of issues and opportunities when they should focus their time and attention. Remember to respect their time as much as you respect your own time and the time of your boss.

5. Always prepare for your meetings in advance (have a meeting agenda and pre-read materials if required) and be on time – demand the same from the other participants.

6. Remember that managing your time is not just managing your calendar. It also includes what you do and discuss at your meetings. Every interaction counts.

7. Operate an effective personal productivity system and demand the same from others. We have found Getting Things Done ('GTD') by David Allen to be particularly effective, but there are others that can be useful too.

8. Remember that you cannot plan for everything, so keep a degree of flexibility in your daily schedule anyway. Almost all good personal productivity systems allow for this.

Potential Pitfalls

Unless you have an iron discipline, it is easy to get distracted and be pulled from pillar to post. If you do, don't fret but reprioritise as quickly as possible. Enlist the help of your boss or your team if necessary.

There will always be people who do not respect the time of others and like to abuse it. If this sounds like your boss, then it is easy to get discouraged. Unfortunately, there is little you can do about it but be prepared for it, so when your time is abused, you're not thrown completely off board.

18. Energy Management: How to Manage Your Energy Effectively

Issue: Failure to manage your energy wisely always results in mental and physical exhaustion.

Everyone knows that overwhelming feeling which can lead to tiredness, lower motivation, and indifference to your work. The presence of such feelings allows negativity and cynicism to set in and reduce even further your professional efficacy. Despite your best intentions, you can easily become overwhelmed if you fail to understand the root cause of these feelings.

The root of poor energy management is simple: the more incomplete commitments that you have, the more energy-depleted you will feel. The key word here is 'incomplete'. The reason for this phenomenon is that your sub-conscious mind fastidiously keeps track of your commitments and allocates energy to them. The longer they remain incomplete, the more energy you will lose. Note that your sub-conscious mind does not differentiate between work commitments or personal commitments. That is why your work life can have a negative bearing on your personal life and vice versa.

Many people don't realise what is causing their lack of energy and blame their company, their boss, the market conditions, or anything else they can point to. The truth is that they, and they alone, are responsible.

For example, many people believe that they cannot say 'no' to their boss because it will make them look bad. This belief is often unfounded. If you keep saying 'yes' to everything your boss throws your way, they will just assume that you can handle it. You must realise that saying 'yes' to everything is a lose-lose proposition for you, your boss, and your company because in the long run, your energy and productivity will suffer. You also must realise that 'yes' and 'no' are not your only options. You also have the options to delegate further or to renegotiate your priorities with your boss.

Principles

Applying the following principles will allow your mind to relax and release some of your blocked energy.

1. You must be crystal clear what your agreed commitments are by keeping all of them in one single place. Usually, our commitments reside in various places: on our computers, on post-it notes, in our wallets, on the fridge door, and most commonly in some part of our minds. Things can get lost when spread in these places; however, the sub-conscious never forgets and will allocate energy to them, even when our conscious mind has forgotten about them. Hence, it is imperative to take all commitments out of our sub-conscious mind and store them into our conscious mind by writing them down in one place.

2. You should never accept new commitments if they don't support your priorities, as per the principles and actions outlined in the previous two chapters.

3. If circumstances change and you can't keep any of your existing commitments, you should either renegotiate them with your boss or reprioritise them (i.e., free up some time by renegotiating something else). Time is a fixed constraint.

Actions

There are a number of actions that could be considered:

1. While consolidating all your existing commitment in one place, the following will also help you enormously:

- Classify commitments in logical groups, e.g., work and personal, project by project, by functionality, etc.
- Assign priorities by linking to or deriving from the Management Agenda and applying the principles outlined in the previous chapter.

- Drop immediately all commitments that do not support your priorities and that you have no intention of doing. This will give you an immediate mental and physical respite and an energy boost.

2. If you are a manager and you can delegate commitments to people working for you, you should always delegate (not abdicate) all that you can – subject to a conversation and an agreed commitment. Thus, it will fall off your plate and release your energy. The only thing you should be concerned about afterwards is when to follow up.

3. Each commitment that cannot be effectively delegated must be associated with a concrete timeframe. This will allow you to find a time in your calendar to work on it. Some people prefer to set specific times for specific commitments, while others prefer to keep large blocks of time free and work on whatever is most pressing at that time. It's up to you.

4. At all times, keep the following easily accessible:
- The Blueprint (as the fuselage for the company's approach to work)
- The Value Goals
- The Risk Appetite Statement
- The Management Agenda
- The Company's Strategy
- The MTP
- The Budget for the Current Year
- The Decision Rules

5. You should track your own and delegated commitments religiously. The best way to do this is to keep a diarised daily tracking system for:
- Personal commitments
- Team commitments e.g., your/their objectives and commitments, and personal & professional development plans

6. Keep a dedicated time in your diary to plan for the next week. It's up to you when you do this. Of the authors, one of us likes to do so on Friday afternoon, and the other prefers Sunday evening.

7. Finally, you should always be in communication with your boss and your team, as there will always be times that commitments have to be renegotiated.

Potential Pitfalls

The inability or the unwillingness to say 'no' to new commitments is the main reason why people get physically and mentally exhausted at work. Below are some of the reasons why. If you recognise any of the below, stop, reflect, and change the underlying behaviour.

- The hero syndrome – I'm going to do it alone as heroes do, no matter what it takes. This is a popular Hollywood paradigm that we all have been subjected to.

- The perfectionist syndrome – I'm going to prove that I am the best (or keep all the balls in the air), no matter what it takes and deliver everything. It's like the hero syndrome but the underlying motivation is the drive for perfection.

- The busy fool syndrome – I'm going to keep busy to fool myself and others as to my importance. That is quite popular among people with low self-esteem who rely on being busy to prove their worth to themselves and the world. Usually, they focus completely on the wrong things.

- The pet project syndrome – I'm going to focus on what matters to me and me alone. This is a purely narcissistic motivation. The irony is that it might not exhaust the person that employs it, but it will exhaust everyone else around them.

- The dart board syndrome – I'm going to scatter my energies on a million different things in the hope that one might land. This is quite common among newly promoted managers who are still not clear what their priorities should be.

- The FOMO (Fear of Missing Out) syndrome – I'm going to get as involved as possible in everything that I can because I don't want to be left out. This is, again, driven by deep personal insecurity.

As a leader it is very important to create a culture where those with the courage to say 'no' or renegotiate for the right reasons are not perceived as being uncommitted, poor team players, or penalised as under-performers. It is all part of creating an environment of 'speaking truth to power.'

SECTION 4: MANAGING OTHERS

Managing others is a key topic in leadership. For a long time in business there had been two key levers to direct the behaviour of others: pay and punishment. Indeed, this approach dates back to antiquity. The emperors of long forgotten empires either bought loyalty or crushed into submission those who stood in their way. Fortunately, we have been outgrowing this phase in human evolution and this is very noticeable in the corporate world nowadays.

The emphasis of many leaders has shifted from 'I am the most important person here' to 'My people are more important than me'. Caring about others, being of service to others, fostering personal development and co-operation, and maintaining an environment of psychological safety have all become daily requirements in a leader's world. It has been proven time and again that such attitudes and actions enhance the performance of teams and individuals way beyond the blunt approach of 'pay and punishment'.

Therefore, management in the twenty-first century represents the art of getting things done through others, without exploitation, alienation, fear, threats, etc. Pay is still an important lever of getting the right people through the door and motivating performance, but it is not the primary driver, and never has been. Punishment also still exists, but it is becoming rarer to threaten someone with a reprimand just to get them to do something. Even the ultimate punishment – the layoff – when unavoidable (normally because of under-performance or economic restructuring) should be handled with care.

Section 4 is organised as follows:

Chapter 19 discusses the issue of Sourcing and Selecting the best people for your company. Finding the best people is not an easy process. As a matter of fact, it is extremely costly and time-consuming, making hiring mistakes some of the most expensive in business.

Leading Without Winging It

Chapter 20 addresses embedding a high-performing team in an effective manner. In collective sports, it is well known that a loose collection of very good individual players does not automatically make a very good team. The same is true in business. Despite a rigorous hiring process aimed at finding the best candidates, some can still prove to be incompatible with the rest of the team. The onboarding process is where this risk is minimised further.

Chapter 21 discusses how to deal with complex stakeholders, such as Boards and Regulatory Bodies. Large companies routinely deal with many stakeholders whose interests may contradict with the interest of the owners. Knowing how to interact with such stakeholders is a key leadership skill.

Chapter 22 is dedicated to managing performance effectively. Both informal feedback and formal performance management conversations are very important for any company. Without them, no one will know whether they are doing a good job and whether they should be making any changes to their behaviours and actions.

Chapter 23 discusses Reward and Recognition as a source of competitive advantage. It should be recognised that Reward is much broader in scope than just remuneration. Unless it is also used this way, its full potential to motivate and inspire employees will be lost to the company. Recognition, on the other hand, is distinctly different from Reward and has its own important role to play as well.

Chapter 24 discusses the requirement of leaders to switch between different management styles, dependent on the situation. Authoritarian (Theory X) and Participative (Theory Y) styles of management are both rooted in the assumptions leaders make about their employees and the situations they find themselves in. Clearly, neither all employees nor all situations are the same. Therefore, leaders must adapt their management styles according to context – yet too many senior executives are unable to do so.

Chapter 25 addresses how to manage in a crisis. A crisis is something that breaks down corporate routines abruptly. It cannot be dealt with through the normal Operating Rhythm and decision-making processes. Therefore, leadership must adopt a discrete set of principles, processes, and decision-making rules to overcome the crisis and minimise the potential damage.

Chapter 26 discusses the issue of silent disagreement at senior management and executive levels of a company. Silent disagreement arises when people are afraid to speak up openly. It could be an attribute of the company's culture or a result of the leadership's intimidating style. In any case, if it is not addressed explicitly, it could create a toxic environment of passive-aggressive behaviours.

Chapter 27 is about recognising stress in others and dealing with it effectively. There is no doubt that stress is an unavoidable side effect of being alive. Excessive stress, however, can lead to many undesirable consequences. It is the leader's duty to take care of their team members, and this includes recognising when they are exposed to excessive stress. Here we discuss the typical stress-coping mechanisms that people adopt at work and how to reduce intentionally their negative side-effects.

Chapter 28 examines the displays of narcissistic behaviours at work. Some people's tendency for such behaviours can cause enormous harm to the working environment. The leader should know how to distinguish the 'corporate narcissists' from the talented and results-orientated people in their team and understand how to deal with the issue effectively.

Chapter 29 is dedicated to dealing with interpersonal rivalry, which is very common in the corporate world. Even though some competition among team members is healthy as it pushes people to improve, when taken to an extreme, it can become destructive for the working environment. It can lead to lost productivity and other significant long-term costs.

Leading Without Winging It

Chapter 30 discusses the issue of letting people go. Dismissing an employee can be an emotional and agonising process for both sides. Hence, many leaders resist letting people go at all costs. Unfortunately, it is an inevitable part of corporate life. The more the decision is delayed, the more painful and costly it is going to be. Here we discuss the principles of letting people go without complication and emotional drama.

19. Recruitment: How to Source and Select the Best People

Issue: Hiring mistakes are some of the costliest in business.

The hiring process at most companies is not geared towards finding and keeping A-players – which is somewhat disconcerting when surely a leader's number one priority is to surround themselves with the very best people.[11]

No matter how sophisticated they appear, most hiring processes are essentially a gamble. Despite management's best intentions, hiring processes fail more often than they succeed. Below are some of the common reasons why:

- Hiring managers are not clear enough about: the purpose of the open roles; the outcomes/results required from those hired; the necessary capabilities to perform the job; and, how to test the candidates effectively for good cultural fit.
- Hiring managers do not apply consistency in the hiring process across the organisation, which makes it difficult to compare candidates objectively for different roles.
- Hiring managers often tend to recruit people who are more like them, which over stifles diversity of thought.
- Hiring managers often commit mistakes during interviews, which significantly jeopardise the desired outcome of hiring A-players.

---

[11] An A-Player is defined as somebody who is in the top 10 per cent of the available candidates.

- Hiring managers sometimes carry certain bad hiring habits from one job to another, which go uncorrected throughout their careers.
- Hiring managers recruit too hastily instead of taking their time and doing it correctly – normally caused by the day-to-day pressures of work.

It's clear that hiring mistakes are very costly in terms of recruitment costs, training costs, lost productivity, not building a diverse workforce, etc. It is something that most senior executives would like to avoid and yet they keep committing the same mistakes time and again.

We have certainly committed the same mistakes many times during our careers. In one of the companies that we used to work for, the CEO had to reconstitute the ExCo from scratch. All positions were announced as open and internal and external candidates were invited to apply. There was big pressure from both from the regulatory body and the Board of Directors to fill these positions as soon as possible. This is what led to the first hiring mistake: the CEO felt pressed to hire the senior executives hastily. Some of those new hires were indeed A-players, but for those who were not, the whole company paid a high price later.

The second hiring mistake, which became glaringly obvious over time, was that we didn't do any cultural fit assessment as part of the hiring process. What the CEO needed was senior executives who shared the principles and beliefs for how the company should be managed, e.g., the importance of having Governing Objectives, a Management Agenda, etc. Unfortunately, some of the people who were hired did not share those principles and beliefs, which became the source of many problems later.

Principles

There are a number of principles that must be applied:

1. Who you hire is more important than whether the candidate has the perfect set of capabilities to do the job. That is, the 'who' is more important than the 'what'. It does not matter if you're hiring someone externally or promoting someone from within – you still want an A-player in the job. The definition of 'who' is much broader than the requirements of the job. It

includes character, attitudes, beliefs, ability to get along with others, etc. We have all made the mistake of hiring the perfect candidate in terms of qualifications and capabilities only to discover later that they had a major character defect. Good examples of the right mindset are private equity companies, which have been betting on the principle of 'A-players' for a long time. They have always known that if the initial business plan was 'off-track', a team of A-players would pivot and produce great results.

2. Establishing a sound and tested hiring process maximises the chance of hiring A-players. One must always bear in mind that A-players are difficult to find, and the process is always likely to take some time. We prefer a mix of psychometric testing; panel interviews (using a diverse panel); a 'Who' interview (see below); a full and frank debate between panel members so all views are aired and debated; and, critically, broad and deep reference checks.

3. In the case of senior hires, there is always a debate about the value of Specialists vs. Generalists. We believe that senior leaders should have the skills and capabilities of both, i.e., to be a technical leader in their field but complemented by the skills of general management – the primacy of managing for Owner Value; strategy development; resource allocation; managing by agenda; corporate finance; sourcing, selecting and leading people, etc. It is critical that the selection process tests for both dimensions. One without the other is not good enough.

Actions

In terms of sound and tested hiring process, we strongly recommend 'the A Method' by Geoff Smart.[12] This recommendation is based on long, painful, and costly experiences with many different in-house hiring processes at various companies.

The A Method establishes a four-step process for hiring:
- Scorecard: Create a Scorecard for each position
- Source: Create a pipeline of high-quality candidates
- Select: Conduct a series of structured interviews

---

[12] Geoff Smart and Randy Street, *Who: The A Method for Hiring*, Ballantine Books, 1st edition, 2008.

- Sell: Persuade the high-quality people to join as they often have many options on the table

We must emphasise a few important points from the A Method:

- Scorecards describe the core purpose of the position, the outcomes that must be accomplished by the candidate, and the competencies that fit with both the culture of the company and the role. The Scorecard must be explicitly linked to the company's Strategy and Management Agenda. The Scorecard must be iterated over time as the Strategy and Management Agenda evolves – this is a good way of testing to ensure the right person is in the role on a continuous basis (as company needs and individual competences may diverge over time).

- Outcomes describe what a person needs to accomplish in a role. An A-player will be able to accomplish the desired outcomes, but a B- or C-player won't. Thus, the outcomes must be stretching, linked to the Management Agenda, and, if possible, quantitative.

- Competencies are assessed against how you expect a new hire to operate in the fulfilment of the job and the achievement of the outcomes.

- Cultural fit is assessed against the Company's Governing Objective, Vision, and Management Model.

The interview process is made up of four layers:

- Screening Interview: Separates those who have the potential to be A-players from the rest.

- The WHO Interview®: Walks a candidate in-depth through their career, collecting as many facts as possible to support the assessment (undertaken by the Hiring Manager and an experienced 'WHO' interviewer).

- Focused Interview: Tests the candidate against the outcomes and competencies of the Scorecard (a good place to use other Panel Members).

- Reference Interview: References deeply to verify what was heard in the previous interviews.

Despite how good this method is, we have learnt the hard way that for it to be successful, it must be fully endorsed by the CEO, the HR Director, and the entire senior executive team.

Potential Pitfalls

As always, there are some pitfalls to be aware of:

1. Hiring is not made a top priority of the organisation. No matter how sophisticated one's hiring process is, unless it is made a top priority, it is unlikely to produce the desired outcomes.

2. There is no clear link between the Job Scorecard and the company's Strategy and Management Agenda. Any job without such a link must not exist in the first place.

3. Hiring managers are not trained in the 'WHO' process and are allowed to carry over automatically bad hiring and interviewing habits.

4. Failure to recognise and reward exceptionally good hiring managers. In every organisation there are people who make consistently better hiring decisions than others. They must be recognised and rewarded.

5. Ironically, the biggest danger to establishing a sound and tested hiring process comes from the HR team itself, as people working in this function have the most established habits and practices. They must buy into following the 'WHO' hiring process from the very beginning and become its owners. In our experience, this is a really difficult conversation which may require a more directive approach.

20. High-Performing Teams: How to Embed High-Performing Teams

Issue: A collection of high-performing A-players does not automatically constitute a high-performing team.

No matter how good the recruitment and selection process there is always a chance of getting it wrong. Although this risk cannot ever be completely eradicated, it can be minimised as we described in Chapter 19. Everyone we hire brings their own personal history and pre-existing ideas, assumptions, and biases about the world and others around them. Despite rigorous testing and interviewing, it may still turn out that a person is incompatible with the Governing Objective, Vision, or Management Model. This does not mean that they are a bad or incompetent – it just means that they don't fit properly with the Blueprint for the individual organisation.

There are certainly many things that we can do to minimise this element of the recruitment risk. Of course, selecting and recruiting a potential A-player is the first step where we should test the competencies associated with teamwork and collaboration. The second step is just as important: they need to be on-boarded into the team in a way that maximises both individual and team performance. In this regard, it is the role of the leader to build and gel the team together. Getting this wrong could mean the team ends up like those soccer teams that, on paper, have all the best players, yet fail to win the most coveted trophies.

Let's illustrate this with a couple of examples. The first example is of a candidate with an impressive CV who did very well in the interviews for a senior executive role. The impression made was of a person who cared in equal measure about the quality of the work and team members. Unfortunately, during the recruitment process the interviewers failed to spot a very specific drawback: the love of gossiping with everyone about everyone else. Gossip is incompatible with high performance. Perhaps it wouldn't have been a problem if the rules of high-performance teams (especially the elements of the Management Model) were explained at the very beginning through a proper onboarding process and commitment to the Blueprint from the onset. Unfortunately, they were not, and the person had to be let go after several embarrassing gaffes with colleagues.

The second example is a candidate who was recruited after a very long search. Candidates with the required specific expertise were in short supply in the market. When the person appeared on the horizon as a potential candidate, the recruitment manager instantly decided to hire. As a result, the recruitment process was not as rigorous as it should have been. Despite the candidate being a A-player on paper, it turned out that the person was a political animal who saw corporate life as a game to be played amongst colleagues based on maximising personal positioning, creating political alliances, and ingratiating themself with key stakeholders – all at the expense of maximum focus on value creation. Proper on-boarding and a rigorous introduction as to how the existing team worked would have maximised potential. Instead, the person was left to build coalitions, which is what politically astute people do. After six to eight months, the person had already generated severe factions and unhealthy relationships, which led to number of undesired departures.

Principles

Knowing Your Team

Every leader who cares about the performance of their team must care about each individual member of the team in equal measure. One way that this manifests in daily life is through knowing everyone's personal circumstances, such as their strengths and weaknesses, the names of their partners and their children, significant events in their lives, what motivates or scares them, etc. A good place to start is a detailed career conversation, supported by psychometric tests – aka the selection and recruitment process.

This 'personal factual matrix' can then be complemented by an in-depth analysis of the team; by way of example, a tool such as Hogan Team will aggregate individual data to create a view of likely team dynamics.

This knowledge should then be purposefully replenished during the time you spend together. It must be noted that knowing a lot of personal details about the people on your team does not require friendship, but it does presume personal care.

Alignment Behind the Governing Objective, Vision, and Management Model

The Governing Objective, Vision, and Management Model represent the formal boundaries for the high-performing team or organisation. It is the Blueprint that everyone should study and apply in daily work life. It defines the common Value Goal, common processes, common values, common behaviours, and the structure that everyone should follow. Hence, it is imperative that all team members are aligned behind it from the very beginning.

Again, the selection and recruitment process should weed out those with fundamentally different beliefs while respecting diversity of thought. In addition, and this can appear brutal, any early signs of misalignment should be managed quickly, otherwise the virus of silent disagreement will seep through the organisation.

Psychological Safety

Psychological safety is defined as 'a shared belief held by members of a team that the team is safe for interpersonal risk taking'; that is, the work environment feels safe without limiting self-expression or censoring what they say or do due to a fear of punishment.[13] Creating an environment of psychological safety is completely within the responsibilities of the leader. Authoritarian leadership tends to have exactly the opposite effect, and that's another reason why it fails

---

[13] As defined by organisational behavioural scientist Amy Edmondson in the paper 'Psychological Safety and Learning Behavior in Work Teams' (1999).

in the long run. Hence, practicing the participative style of management (see Chapter 24), knowing your team, and aligning behind the Governing Objective, Vision, and Management Model construct creates the right conditions for psychological safety.

Recurring Process

Every team evolves over time. Some people leave and others join. People's behaviours and attitudes change. The challenges facing the team change. Hence, building the team and keeping it on the path of high performance never ends. The worst thing that can happen is for the leader to decide that their job is done and become complacent. They should never forget that their key responsibility is to create and maintain the conditions for high performance for their team as the agent of the owners of the business.

Actions

There are a number of actions that could be considered:

1. Select and recruit based on the Blueprint. For the leader, the selection and recruitment process is a key step in ensuring alignment around the Blueprint. The 'WHO' methodology should be used to ensure that the candidate's core values and beliefs align with the Blueprint while ensuring diversity of thought within the framework is respected and encouraged. For an existing team, we recommend that each member is subject to a 'WHO' interview such that the leader understands the starting point in terms of alignment.

2. Study the interview notes and psychometrics. For the leader, getting to know their team members begins before they have formally joined the company. You should study their interview notes and psychometric tests in detail, drawing conclusions about strengths and areas for improvement. One of the first things that you need to do once they join the team is share the test results and have your team member reflect in their own words. This will deepen your own understanding and ignite their ability for self-reflection. This could also be accompanied by wide-ranging conversation aimed at getting to know them better.

In addition, we recommend that you commission a separate team assessment to provide the baseline for grounding team dynamics.[14]

3. Organise a formal onboarding process (training, compliance, briefings). We are convinced that every single new joiner must go through an onboarding process. When starting a new job, people usually join with a very open mind. This is the single best opportunity to share critical information. If the new joiner is a senior manager or an executive, this is the time and place to reinforce the Governing Objective, the Vision, and the Management Model followed by a mutual commitment to these critical foundations.

4. Create an environment of psychological safety. The concept of psychological safety became prominent in management science circles with Google's Project Aristotle.[15] They looked at 180 of their teams (both high- and low-performing teams) to identify the team dynamics that contributed most to the team's effectiveness.

Based on our experience, we came to understand that psychological safety is created through building and maintaining the conditions that allow it to flourish. These conditions might vary according to the circumstances, e.g., the severity and the urgency of the issues at hand, but in general those conditions include:

- Aligning behind the Management Model, i.e., the rules of working together
- Practicing a participative management style (see Chapter 24)
- Practicing inclusion – everyone on the team matters and everyone is heard
- Practicing Radical Candor™ conversations (see Chapter 22)
- Practicing Effective Decision-Making (see Chapter 6)

Potential Pitfalls

There are several important pitfalls that one must be aware of and manage effectively.

---

[14] Such as the Hogan Team Report.
[15] To learn more just search for Project Aristotle in Google.

Leading Without Winging It

1. Interpersonal Rivalry. The souring of individual relationships will hinder the performance of the whole team. Hence, it is important to address interpersonal rivalry as soon as one becomes aware of it. We have addressed the issue in more detail in Chapter 29.

2. Silent Disagreement. Silent disagreement is rooted in the absence of psychological safety. The problem is that by its nature it might be difficult to detect. It is an important issue, which we have described in more detail in Chapter 26.

3. Accusations of Preferential Treatment. Leading a high-performing team can sometimes be likened to being a parent. Everyone is focused on you and every action of yours is either imitated or criticised. If you happen to have a closer personal or professional relationship with someone else on the team, it can sometimes lead to accusations of preferential treatment, which itself can turn into resentment.

It is important to address those accusations as soon as you become aware of them, and not allow them to turn into resentment. First, you need to take a step back and ask yourself: 'Do these accusations have any merit?' If the answer is 'yes', you should correct your behaviours. If the answer is 'no', then you should examine the root cause of the issue by gathering facts and concrete examples.

If the issue lies with the behaviours of the person that you are closer to (for example, they misuse the relationship to pursue their own ends), then you need to have an honest conversation with them based on the principles of Radical Candor™.

If the issue lies with the team (for example, they regard the person you are closer to as competition or as an outsider), then you must openly work with the team to address the issue head-on. This is where alignment with the Management Model and ways of working is going to be critical, as these rules must apply to everyone.

4. Silo Mentality. Oftentimes a long-standing team, such as a whole department or a whole support function, can start seeing themselves as better than the rest of the company – with different language, different behaviours,

and different ways of doing things. This is a serious cultural issue that can lead to under-performance across the board.

In our experience, this does not happen coincidentally, but rather it is always initiated by the manager of the group. It is often accompanied by interpersonal rivalry with another manager of a similar group. Your job as the leader is to identify what is happening and take corrective action as soon as possible by applying the principles outlined in Chapter 29.

21. Complex Stakeholders: How to Deal with Regulators and Boards

Issue: Dealing with complex stakeholders is never an easy task and requires specific leaderships skills.

Large companies routinely deal with many stakeholders whose interests may contradict the interests of the companies' owners. Almost by definition, none of the decisions made by company leadership will ever satisfy all stakeholders equally. This is why the establishment of a Governing Objective is so important – it guides decision-making like a North Star in a maze of conflicting interests and demands on the company's resources.

However, there are also other stakeholders who hold significant influence over the company's activities and decisions, and whose interests do not necessarily wholly align with those of the owners. These could be, for example, regulatory bodies, the Stock Exchange, parliamentary commissions, supranational organisations such as the IMF, etc.

There is also another type of stakeholder whose interests should, at least in theory, be aligned with those of the owners but may not because the interests of individual members might diverge. A good example is the Board of Directors, which is supposed to behave and make decisions homogeneously (this does not mean unanimously); however, in our experience, individual interests (or disinterests), (flawed) beliefs, and capital market inexperience might easily take over.

Company leaders must deal effectively with all these stakeholder types on a regular basis. This chapter is dedicated specifically to dealing with Regulators and Boards; however, the principles described here are applicable to a much broader set of complex stakeholders.

Regulatory Bodies

Regulators are mandated to protect the public good. They are tasked with preventing abuse of corporate power and protecting vulnerable groups, the economy, and the environment. Some industries are monitored by multiple Regulators at the same time.

By definition, the Regulators' interests are not aligned with those of shareholders. However, we think about this in a clear way. Even though we know that creating shareholder value is the most important objective of any company, it must not be created at the expense of vulnerable groups, economic volatility, or damaging the environment. The way to align the interests of the company and the public good is to treat the needs of influential – but not equal - stakeholders as inputs to the company's strategy development process rather than ignoring them or treating them as side-effects or outputs. In this way, they can act as input constraints to what is possible for the company, not as conflicting objectives. See Chapter 3 for a more detailed discussion.

Of course, Regulators adopt a contrarian/policing approach to regulation – in most cases justifiably – because their basic assumption is that companies will behave against the public good if not kept in check. Responding and adapting to such an approach is a key leadership skill and is based on a set of principles laid out below.

Boards

In theory, a company's Board should protect the interest of the owners. Again, the reality is often quite different. Board members come from different personal and career backgrounds. Often their own personal interests and beliefs take precedence over the interests of the owners', and this creates on-going challenges for any leader whose core belief is based on the creation of sustainable shareholder value as a Governing Objective.

Another challenge is when Board members do not have the necessary knowledge, expertise, or indeed capability to be effective Board members – which is where there must be total alignment between Chair and CEO on the

Governing Objective. Unfortunately, the lack of understanding of the Governing Objective, corporate finance, Customer Value management, etc, happens surprisingly often, even in heavily regulated industries where a fitness and probity test must be passed before being appointed to the Board.

Dealing effectively with Board members is a key leadership skill. Unsurprisingly, it is based on the same set principles.

Principles

The first thing to recognise when dealing with complex stakeholders is that a contrarian or antagonistic approach is unlikely to work for obvious reasons. One needs a structured and systematic approach that is also long term in nature. This is one area of leadership where winging it is not advisable.

1. Define the Rules of Engagement

The first key principle is to define clear rules of engagement with each complex stakeholder as early as possible in the relationship. This should be a continuous rather than a one-off process. It must be done every time there is a change of personnel on either side of the relationship – whether it's a new incoming CEO, a new Board member, or a change in the Regulatory oversight team. Any such change must be seen as an opportune moment to refresh everyone's understanding of how the relationship is supposed to work and its outer boundaries.

Rules of engagement typically cover three areas: (i) clear articulation of respective core beliefs, (ii) delineation of roles and responsibilities, and (iii) setting of an Operating Rhythm.

Core Beliefs

We are clear one of the benefits of a codified 'Blueprint' is that it leaves no ambiguity for stakeholders as to the core foundations of a company, e.g.:

- Governing Objective
- Vision (Purpose, Values, Behaviours)
- Management Model (including strategy development standards and Decision Rules)

In this way, there can be no ambiguity as to how each party approaches difficult conversations. Of course, it is important to recognise that, in the case of a Regulator, the company's licence to do business could be at stake.

Roles and Responsibilities

There must be clear delineation between roles and accountabilities of the stakeholder body (i.e., individual members representing it), and the company (i.e., its leadership). There must also be no doubt where the boundaries lie. These boundaries must be codified and discussed.

When the boundaries are challenged or even broken, there must be a process to address such issues openly and without any delay. Such a conflict resolution process – through voting, escalation, or else – is very important for having effective rules of engagement.

For example, a Regulator would be responsible for setting and policing the industry regulations, whereas the company would be responsible for following them. At the same time, the Regulator is not responsible for setting the company's strategy, prioritising activities, allocating resources, or carrying performance reviews of its managers.

In our experience, the 'Shadow Director' principle is a clear and present danger that must be managed with care, respect, and professionalism for all stakeholders – and with the courage to debate and challenge.

Operating Rhythm

Setting an Operating Rhythm is just as important as defining roles and responsibilities. It should be nested within the broader Operating Rhythm of the company (see Chapter 12 for more details). It should include regular meetings with the relevant stakeholders under a standardised agenda based on absolute transparency, drawn up in accordance with the roles and responsibilities of each party. Such an agenda will keep the conversation both focused and structured.

2. Establish an Environment of Trust

Working towards establishing trust in the relationship can only happen within the rules of engagement. The rules of engagement represent the framework within which trust can be allowed to emerge over time. The goal is to create a safe space for communication and interaction for all parties. It might not happen automatically or quickly, but as leaders you must keep working on it within what you can control.

This principle is made up of three elements: (i) establish personal relationships, (ii) communicate with transparency, and (iii) be open-minded.

Establish Personal Relationships

First, one must recognise that words like 'Board' and 'Regulator' are abstract nouns used to describe a function performed by a collective of individuals. Abstract nouns do not have personalities, likes and dislikes, or emotions. As such, one cannot possibly establish a relationship of trust with an abstract noun. This can only be done with another individual.

So, our advice is to get to know the people involved on a personal level within the boundaries and the Operating Rhythm that have already been set. This means learning as much as possible about the other person – e.g., their beliefs, professional background, accomplishments, etc. – to enable you to relate to each other as individuals, not just as representatives of your respective abstract nouns.

Communicate with Transparency

Second, within the agreed rules of engagement, one should communicate with complete transparency. This means that issues must be addressed head-on, and information should be shared proactively and in a timely manner. Only with complete transparency does trust build.

Practice Open-Mindedness

Third, one must approach the contributions of the other party with an open mind. This could be hard to do if you think that members of the Regulatory team or the Board do not have either the experience or the knowledge and expertise that you bring to the table. Nevertheless, you should remain open and inquisitive about their contributions. Being respectful, having patience, and not acting defensively are key. That said, one must reserve the right to 'push back' if the rules of engagement boundaries are blurred or crossed.

Actions

Keeping in mind the above principles, let's look at some of the possible actions that could be taken when dealing with Regulators and Boards.

Regulators

In a regulated business, there is no more important stakeholder than the 'Regulator'. The 'Regulator' (writ large) can take many forms. Prudential, Conduct, Data, and Ombudsman are just a few broad examples from the banking industry.

The importance of a disciplined Management Model cannot be understated in shaping the regulatory dialogue, as sometimes there may have to be trade-offs made on both sides to maintain the integrity of the Governing Objective. Indeed, we cannot stress enough that, by maintaining the primacy of the shareholder, there is a clear 'stake in the ground' for regulatory debates. In simple terms, the role of the CEO is to ensure that any regulatory intervention does not compromise the Governing Objective or, at least, is the basis for any trade-off.

In all cases, the underlying principle is one of 'transparency'. It is critical that the CEO sets the tone in terms of balancing respect, full information sharing, meeting deadlines, and regular dialogues whilst holding the ground in terms of the Governing Objective, managing by agenda, and the commercial imperative.

In terms of Operating Rhythm, we have found that it works best to schedule regular dialogue sessions with the Regulator and use those events to share the company's Management Agenda, Financial Plan, and Performance KPIs.

In addition, the regular inspection calendar of the Regulator is an enormously useful intervention in terms of helping build the strategic factbase. In our experience in the banking industry, the Regulator's interventions across all areas of a bank (e.g., Capital, Liquidity, Risk Management, Business Model, Culture, Remuneration, etc.) are enormously helpful in shaping the Management Agenda. The leadership skill here is to work with the Regulator, adopt the principle of open-mindedness, agree priorities and trade-offs, and never be defensive.

In summary, the Regulator is a critical stakeholder and, at most times, a very useful 'outside in' source of check and challenge to the Board and ExCo. The key is to agree an Operating Rhythm based on transparency and work with the Regulator for the betterment of the company while retaining the right to 'push back' if lines are blurred or crossed.

Boards

From the very beginning of their tenure, the CEO must be clear about what they 'stand for' and how the company will be run. Without this alignment, the relationship with the Board is doomed.

The CEO must explain to the members of the Board in as much detail as possible the key beliefs and practices that they are going to follow. Based on this book, we recommend these three domains:

- Governing Objective
- Vision
- Management Model

While it is important that the CEO sets the outer boundaries (as per above), they must respect the right of the Chairman and the Board members to contribute based on their experience and expertise.

In addition, formal roles and responsibilities must be drawn between the Board and the company's ExCo, as well as between the CEO and the Chairman. The best practice is to do this by writing up formal Terms of Reference, which draw very specific lines of delineation.

Once the boundaries have been set, the CEO (with the support of ExCo and, in particular, the CFO and CSO), should agree on an Operating Rhythm. This must include embedding an annual Board Strategy Away Day where the factbase and strategy alternatives are debated, and alignment is achieved on the Management Agenda and Financial Plan (see Chapter 6 for more details). These then become the key accountabilities of the CEO and ExCo for the performance year.

Leading Without Winging It

The Chairman hires and fires the CEO, so it is important to agree on an Operating Rhythm for this relationship. The underlying principle is always transparency around both rational and emotional domains. Based on our experience, we recommend that the Chairman and CEO undertake a regular (weekly) one-to-one meeting, where progress against the Management Agenda is reported together with any other issues and opportunities which might require debate and counsel.

The relationship between the CEO and the Company Secretary is also very important as the Board's (and its sub-committee's) own Operating Rhythm is critical to the successful running of the company. The CEO should own the Agenda and the Papers of all meetings and set the standard in terms of quality and consistency.

The regular Board meeting is one of the most important meetings in the corporate calendar. Both the Chairman and CEO must spend good time together in agreeing on the agenda, the timings, the choreography, and the target outcomes. The CEO should pre-wire the Chairman with the highest-value papers to ensure there is support in principle.

It is also critical that the Chairman provides inclusive leadership and an environment of psychological safety in the Boardroom. In fact, we would argue this was one of the most important conditions for the success of any company. Being able to talk freely without fear of judgement or reprisal supports constructive debate, idea generation, move to action, and personal/professional growth.

It is the CEO's accountability to set the tone in terms of absolute transparency, balance, and the standards of facts, alternatives, and Decision Rules. We have observed that many talented executives lack the confidence to show themselves and their business 'warts and all' and think the Board is a version of 'show and tell'. The CEO must set the tone from Day Zero.

The CEO must also take the time to build relationships with individual Board members, always respecting that the non-executive directors 'dip in and out' of the company. In this regard, it is important to understand the core business beliefs of each non-executive director and find areas of common ground, again respecting that the role of non-executive directors is to check and challenge.

Finally, it is important that the CEO supports the Chairman in refreshing the Board membership. There should be alignment on the key issues and opportunities facing the company, the core capabilities required, and the recruitment and selection standards.

Pitfalls

As always, when dealing with complex stakeholders such as Regulators and Boards, there are several pitfalls that one must be aware of to navigate successfully.

1. The attitude of the CEO and ExCo is critical. Some may view these complex stakeholders as groups to fight or obfuscate, adopting a mindset of 'you find the information as I'm not sharing voluntarily'. We cannot think of a more incorrect attitude.

2. Certain members of the Board or the Regulatory team can come on board with ill-conceived views on the role of the company (normally, the 'stakeholder view'; see Chapter 1), the positioning of customers (normally, passionate about 'Value To' but deeply uncomfortable with the concept of 'Value From'; see Chapter 7) and the cost of equity capital (normally, a view that it is scarce but free, which in actuality is plentiful but expensive; see Chapter 1 again). Inevitably, patience and time will be required to bring those individuals on a journey and potentially change their minds. If you are unable to do so, exit these individuals dispassionately. The Governing Objective, Vision, and Management Model are the guardrails; diversity and inclusivity play within those rails.

3. In the aftermath of the 2008 global financial crisis, the Regulators – especially in the financial services industry – have become more intrusive and prescriptive. Some independent observers might argue that they have adopted the role of 'Shadow Directors'. This is a dangerous trend. As such, it is one of the biggest challenges to independent company leadership as, inevitably, what might be considered an 'issue or opportunity' by the Regulator might not be aligned with the Board's or Management's view of the highest-value initiatives

for the company. This is a real challenge and requires much thought, resilience, and patience.

4. Finally, another dangerous pitfall for the CEO and ExCo is the attitude of the company's Regulatory & Compliance team. If the team members see themselves as a subsidiary of the Regulator and not an extension of the company's Governing Objective, Vision, and Management Model, then the CEO and ExCo will have a big problem. Therefore, we cannot emphasise enough the importance of recruitment and selection in building the Regulatory & Compliance teams. There must be 100 per cent alignment with how the CEO intends to run the company, otherwise the team will (intentionally or unintentionally) compromise the Management Model. Of course, this must not stop the team articulating the regulatory perspective in an environment of psychological safety.

22. Performance Management: How to Implement It Effectively

Issue: Ineffective performance management can tilt any company off-track and diminish the intrinsic potential of its workforce.

Without a doubt, performance management is extremely important for any organisation. After all, without a proper performance management system, no one will know where they stand or whether they are doing a good job. Moreover, the performance management system serves as an important feedback mechanism to everyone as to whether the company is moving in the right direction towards its Governing Objective and Vision.

For the sake of clarity, we distinguish between three discrete but connected elements linked to performance management and ensuring each colleague is the 'best they can be':

1. Performance Management: the systematic and codified review of a performance period (for example, half and full year reviews). We like the construct of 'Stop/Start/Continue' as a great way of focusing on what matters and recommend the moderation of draft ratings to ensure there is a fair distribution across the company.[16]

2. Performance Feedback: the regular day-to-day conversations that should happen in any high-performing culture; we like the construct of the Radical Candor™ feedback framework for praise and criticism:[17]

- Humble
- Helpful
- Offer guidance in person

---

[16] DeLong, Thomas, 'Three Questions for Effective Feedback', *Harvard Business Review*, August 2011.

[17] Kim Scott, *Radical Candor: How To Get What You Want By Saying What You Mean*, Mcmillan, Main Market Edition, 2017, Chapter 2.

- Praise in public, criticise in private
- Don't personalise

3. Career Conversations: the discrete conversation to understand a colleague's motivations and ambitions (based on understanding a life story, dreams, and plans).

In terms of performance management, an environment where the process is ineffective or does not exist at all can quickly escalate into chaos, which is where survival instincts kick in. In such cases, some people will apply their own standards of what good performance is or is not, while others will shamelessly try to pursue their own objectives. A-players do not thrive in such places and sooner or later they will leave. Even if they decide to stay, without a performance management mechanism (or mechanisms – see above), it is unlikely that such companies can remain competitive over time.

Principles

The below principles should be considered when designing an effective performance management system.

The Equal Importance Principle

Every person in every job in your team or company is equally important. Once you have given them a job, they deserve your attention as much as anyone else, regardless of their actual performance. Not following this principle will quickly compromise the effectiveness of any performance management system. As the old saying goes, 'there is no such thing as an unimportant job or an unimportant person'.

The Cascade Principle

Performance Management must link directly to the Vision and Strategy of the company. Everyone should be able to trace their objectives to the Vision and the Strategy and be able to see how their actual performance contributes to the overall performance of the company. If people can't do that, then they cannot answer the question 'Why' they should do what they've been asked to do, which will leave a significant gap in their motivation.

The Two Dimensions Principle

Objectives should be always set along two dimensions: 'What' is expected from the individual and the 'How' they should do it (based on the Vision – Purpose; Values; Behaviours; Operating Manners). This ensures that there is no ambiguity at the start while at the same time allowing for a more constructive evaluation at the end of the performance management period.

The Radical Candor™ Principle

We love Kim Scott's book *Radical Candor*. The author defines Radical Candor™ as 'what happens when managers show that they care personally for employees while also challenging them directly with clear, kind feedback that is not aggressive or insincere.' Kim recommends accompanying this with getting a good understanding of what motivates each person on your team and creating a culture of open communication and psychological safety.

In our experience, every people manager should be trained in applying Radical Candor™ as part of the feedback process. Even the best conceived performance management systems will fail without Radical Candor™.

The Rockstars and Superstars Principle

This is another principle that we have gladly borrowed from Kim Scott. In the book Kim explains compellingly that there are distinctive sets of A-players: Rockstars and Superstars.

Rockstars are the bedrock of your team. They perform to the highest standard and are consistent and dependable. What distinguishes Rockstars from Superstars is that they are on, what Kim Scott calls, 'a gradual growth trajectory'. This means that they are quite happy where they are in their careers and their place in the corporate hierarchy. They represent a force of stability.

Superstars are also high performers but what makes them different from the Rockstars is their ambition for new challenges and a 'a steep growth trajectory.' They represent a source of change and challenge in your team as they are willing to push the boundaries.

Knowing who you are dealing with is extremely helpful during the Performance Management process as you will be able to provide different challenges and growth opportunities. Also never forget that a Superstar can quite suddenly turn into a Rockstar at certain points in their lives – and the other way around.

In fact, we would go as far to say that having discrete performance management (and Reward) processes for 'Rockstars' and 'Superstars' is a useful construct; in particular, this ensures that focused conversations about 'Rockstars' are not lost during 'Moderation and Reward' sessions. You want both your 'Rockstars' and 'Superstars' to feel valued.

The Self-Awareness Principle

In our experience, self-analysis is a crucial input into the performance management conversation. As a matter of fact, keen awareness of one's own development areas is a key distinguisher of the A-players in your team. We suggest that a great Performance Management process is started by the submission of self-analysis to a manager. We have found this will give you real insight into the mindset of your team – in simple terms, grounded and balanced, delusionary, or closed-minded.

The Under-Performance Principle

Finally, to improve the quality of your team over time means that consistent under-performers must be managed out. The key word here is 'consistent' because even the best sportsmen of all time have had their fair share of bad seasons. Managing people out does not need to be a dreaded prospect if the principle of Radical Candor™ has also been applied consistently.

Actions

Most of the proposed actions follow directly from the principles above.

1. When designing the Performance Management process:
   - Keep it lean – anything greater than one to two pages misses the point
   - Focus on Objectives and Appraisal (do not confuse with Performance Feedback and Career Conversations – see above)

2. When setting Objectives:
- Include 'What' and 'How' as two key dimensions in people's Objectives/ Commitments. We like to call it a Performance Contract
- Link Objectives to the corporate Vision and Strategy. Everyone must know how their work performance contributes to the larger Value Goals of the organisation and their team in particular

3. When performing Appraisals:
- Apply Radical Candor™ and care personally while directly challenging.
- Encourage your team to provide self-analysis ('Stop/Start/Continue' is one possible framework that we have found useful. Another way to approach this might be 'What's Working?'; 'What's Not Working?'; 'What's New and Needed?') in advance of the review against 'Deliverables' and 'Values and Behaviours'. This will give you a clear perspective on your colleague's ability to reflect maturely on their own performance.
- Ensure the Manager drafts a 'Stop/Start/Continue' synopsis in advance of the review.
- Use the Self-Analysis and the manager's 'Stop/Start/Continue' as the raw materials for a 'performance conversation' – we use these words advisedly as there must be a two-way dialogue for the review to be effective. We like to see that the Direct Report and Manager agree on an 'On-Track' vs 'Off-Track' rating against each 'Deliverable' and 'Value/Behaviour'.
- Do not provide an overall rating (even if a 'Draft') until the conclusion of the moderation session. This ensures distributed performance and can enrich the feedback content for the final Manager/Direct Report conversation.
- Differentiate clearly between Rockstars and Superstars and take care of both sets of A-players. Most importantly, consider organising two separate moderation sessions for both categories.

- Make sure there are clear consequences both for met and unmet commitments.

Potential Pitfalls

The biggest pitfall is falling into the bureaucratic trap, making the process long and cumbersome. The key is to develop a system that is lean but honest and avoid the risk of form filling and time consumption exceeding the value of the feedback.

Another noteworthy pitfall is to mix up the three types of conversations: Performance Feedback, Performance Management, and Career Development conversations (again, we must reference that *Radical Candor* by Kim Scott is a fantastic book that could give you more insight into all three elements). These conversions must be clearly separated to avoid creating confusion and sending mixed messages.

23. Reward and Recognition: How to Set Reward and Recognition

Issue: Unless Reward is treated in broader terms, its potential as a source of competitive advantage cannot be fully utilised.

Many leaders view reward in a very narrow way. Usually, it is defined as fixed salary plus any Variable Pay and additional benefits that can be expressed financially, such as a pension or a car allowance. Such a definition ignores a significant component. In our experience, this component is often the main reason why people stick around and don't leave their jobs even if their financial remuneration is less than the market median. It has to do with job satisfaction, the sense of community and belonging, and the recognition that people derive from their job.

One can enjoy a job for many reasons that do not need to be purely financial – the intellectual challenge; the team environment; the comfortable offices; the flexible working support; the presence of a safe psychological environment; the opportunities for advancement; the regular recognition, etc. If leaders do not recognise this, they miss out on an important lever for creating loyalty, employee satisfaction, and, ultimately, an inimitable competitive advantage. The elements of 'Intrinsic' Reward (as opposed to more readily measurable Financial or 'Extrinsic' Reward) are all part of 'creating the best place to work'.

Of course, all components of Reward are extremely important. Extrinsic Reward mainly gets the A-players through the door during the recruitment process, while the Intrinsic Reward elements will keep them in the company for a longer period. It used to be the case that Intrinsic Reward was impossible to compare across companies; however, there are now websites where existing employees share insights from the inside about how rewarding their jobs are. This signifies the rising significance of Intrinsic Reward.

For example, certain companies have long recognised this aspect of Reward and, as a result, their corporate brands already carry that extra attractiveness for jobseekers. There are a few companies like that in almost any industry.

Our own experience is also full of suitable examples. A company that we both used to work for was not particularly well known as a 'best place to work' in the industry, yet one department in this company was able to attract the best people in the market and was never short of internal and external candidates who wanted to work there. Initially, we thought that the reason was the Hiring Manager, but upon closer inspection it turned out there was a combination of factors that increased the attraction of working there: opportunities for continuous learning and development, access to high-level decision-makers, involvement in most important strategic decisions, the pleasure of working with smart colleagues, etc.

Extrinsic Reward

Extrinsic Reward is relatively easy to define as the fixed salary plus variable pay plus other financially quantifiable benefits. The elements of Extrinsic Reward are critical for attracting job candidates as well as for linking both individual and company performance to pay. It is readily comparable across industries, companies, and specific jobs. Hence, it is straightforward for companies to compete for talent along this dimension relatively easily.

Intrinsic Reward

The definition of Intrinsic Reward is slightly trickier. We define it loosely as the presence of an attractive working environment (perhaps characterised by professional and personal value alignment; respect and recognition for the individual; psychological safety; and professional challenge). Some of its most common elements include open and safe communication, a collaborative atmosphere, a competent boss and competent colleagues, and available opportunities for learning and development. It can be difficult to pinpoint strictly the components of an attractive work environment as they may vary by industry and by company. Unlike Extrinsic Reward, Intrinsic Reward can also carry a negative value if the working environment is particularly toxic. It would be difficult to quantify the negative value, although it wouldn't be impossible using metrics such as attrition rates, average tenure, cost of training, cost of strategic and operational mistakes, etc.

Recognition

We are clear that Recognition is distinctly different from Reward. We define Recognition as the timely acknowledgement of actions or work that brings value to the company. We think all leaders should encourage their direct reports to embrace Recognition as a key element of the toolkit – anything from an instant 'thank you' to a handwritten note to small gifts. In addition, we are strong advocates of company-wide recognition schemes.

It's incumbent on the CEO/HRD to develop a 'Recognition Strategy' that is independent of the 'Extrinsic' and 'Intrinsic' reward strategies. The use of 'Recognition' is such a powerful tool in generating connections within the company and between colleagues. In our experience, there is a clear link between recognition and maximising the pool of discretionary effort.

Principles

Consistency Between the Three Elements of Reward

It is important to consider the sum of the elements as Total Reward. Therefore, the three must be consistent with and complementary to each other, as the real competitive advantage is through an integrated approach.

We know that most people will look at both Extrinsic Rewards (i.e., the financial payoff) and Intrinsic Rewards (better work environment) when considering a role. As such, it is a mistake to pay at or above market rates for Extrinsic Reward only to negate this in the Total Reward equation by negative Intrinsic Reward due to operating a toxic working environment. Make sure that, to the largest extent possible, the 'Intrinsic Reward, components can be defined and articulated clearly to A Player candidates.

While the relationship between all components must be a result of a conscious and informed management choice, there is no ready-made formula for how to make this choice. You need A-players to get the balance right.

Linking Total Reward to the Governing Objective

All three components can be expressed in terms of required financial investment, which should only be made if it is expected to produce a return greater than or equal to your company's cost of equity. In other words, it must link back to the company's Governing Objective. This is where the rubber meets the road.

Actions

There are a number of actions that could be considered:

1. It is incumbent on the CEO and HR Director to ensure that there are clear principles and outcomes for all components of the Total Reward Strategy. Each component should be benchmarked on a regular basis, and conscious choices made around competitive positioning and trade-offs should always be underpinned by a high (and differentiated) performance mindset.

2. Based on those principles and outcomes, it should be the job of each individual leader to deliver Intrinsic Reward and Recognition. In our experience, an attractive working environment could be built through:

- Driving collaboration, respect, intellectual curiosity, and continuous learning opportunities
- Understanding the value being created by each person in a team (there are no unimportant people, and there are no unimportant roles)
- Encouraging people to speak 'truth to power'
- Creating meaningful and purposeful work for team members
- Creating a culture of full transparency – share, share, share, unless it is illegal or market-sensitive
- Creating opportunities for further development and promotion
- Providing regular visual and vocal recognition

3. Every year the HR Director should send a statement of Total Reward to each employee with a covering letter from the CEO, which clearly articulates

the employee value proposition. This will allow for the creation of an equity mindset.

4. For Extrinsic Reward, it's critical that all employees understand a few basic principles/default positions:

- The company will allocate a Salary and Bonus Pot each year based on affordability (company performance).
- Salaries will be benchmarked, either individually or as 'job families', to a range – we are used to using 80 per cent to 120 per cent; no colleague should be paid less than 80 per cent or more than 120 per cent (for the latter, the message is simple – accept that your salary will rarely move or find a new role with a different band).
- Salary increases will be allocated based on performance only (as a default position, avoid the 'cost of living' argument as flies in the face of 'performance').
- All things being equal, avoid in-year salary increases and never be held to ransom – no matter how tough the situation, nobody is indispensable as there is always an equal or better resource in the market.
- All things being equal, weigh the balance between Salary and Bonus based on the nature of the roles, e.g., functional roles will have more weighting towards 'fixed' and 'sales' jobs towards 'variable'.
- Bonuses will be allocated based on performance and behaviours only.
- Performance is determined by 'ranking and rating' via the formal Performance Management process; use some form of moderation for both Rockstars and Superstars to achieve a 'bell curve' of distribution.
- If possible, find a way for every 'Colleague' to have equity in the business – through options, a discounted share purchase scheme, a bonus pool linked to equity allocation, etc. Having 'skin in the game' is a key tool to embed the 'Governing Objective'.
- All things being equal, ensure there are 'Malus and Clawback' and 'Good and Bad Leaver' clauses in employment contracts.

Potential Pitfalls

It is very easy to be drawn to the rational Extrinsic element of Reward and undervalue the Intrinsic and Recognition elements. This happens often, and the most common reason is that there is no ready formula for defining, quantifying, and measuring the Intrinsic Reward element.

In addition, leaders who are less motivated by their work environment and more motivated by money also tend to underestimate the value of Intrinsic Reward. Their mistake is to project their own motivation to their entire workforce. Such leaders spend little or no time thinking about how to create the 'best place to work' and forget to ask their team about what matters to them – either individually or collectively.

24. Management Style: Authoritarian or Participative Style?

Issue: Some leaders' inability to adapt their management style to the situation at hand leads to problems in the long run.

The distinction between the authoritarian and participative styles of management was first described in the 1960s by Douglas McGregor in the book *The Human Side of Management.* Many academics and management practitioners have tried to upgrade this model since the 1960s, but McGregor's ideas have remained fundamental. McGregor coined the terms Theory X for authoritarian management style and Theory Y for participative management style. McGregor linked those two 'theories' to the underlying assumptions that managers make about their employees. That is:

* Managers who behave in an authoritarian manner with their employees (Theory X) use a very directive and hands-on approach. They behave this way because they believe fundamentally that their employees do not like to work and have very little innate motivation to do so.
* Managers who employ a more participative management style (Theory Y) use a more collaborative, trusting, and responsibility-based approach. They do so because they believe that their employees are intrinsically motivated to take pride in their work and see it as a positive challenge. They are therefore capable of taking ownership of their work.

Experience tells us that good managers will use both approaches depending on the situational context. Yet it is baffling to see how many managers stick to their default Theory X or Theory Y preference and do not adapt to the context, thus creating many issues both for themselves and the organisation they represent: waste of valuable time and resources, diminished creativity, poor relationships, etc.

In our experience, this happens because their style preference runs much deeper than whether they trust their team members or not.

We have seen that the deeper issue of Theory X advocates is the extent to which they feel secure enough to let go. Many in this category feel compelled to orchestrate the actions and behaviours of others to the minute detail because of their underlying fear of depending on others. They can't clearly see the boundary where colleagues should be allowed to make their own decisions.

We have seen that the deeper issue of Theory Y advocates is their unconscious desire to be liked by the people around them. They feel compelled to include their team members in all the decisions that they are facing. They believe that doing so will make them more likeable. They cannot clearly see the boundary between decisions that should be made by them and decisions that can be delegated. It is ultimately the same boundary but from a different perspective. Ultimately, rigidity in one's management style leads to anxiety and interpersonal issues, which are always accompanied by financial costs.

For example, at one point in our careers, we used to have very close business relationships with several smaller financial services companies that were run by owner-managers. Most of them used the directive management approach, which brought them a lot of success at the beginning because the drive, the connections, and the business acumen of the owner-manager were of crucial importance in the start-up stage. As these companies matured, it became obvious that some of the owners could not switch to a more participative management style because they did not trust their employees. This innate fear of letting go significantly diminished these companies' possibilities for growth over time because it relied on the creativity and capability of only one person. Many of these companies disappeared after the financial crisis of 2008.

Principles

Clear Boundaries for Delegating Decisions

Some companies have their decision boundaries mapped out at every level of the corporate ladder. This is certainly one approach that can be taken. Based on our experience, we have discovered a simpler way, which can be expressed like this: if it can and should be delegated, then delegate. This way, you open time and capacity for yourself to focus on the truly big and important decisions (the Management Agenda). There is a right and wrong way to delegate, though. When delegating, be clear about the expected outcomes, the deadline involved, the dependencies on other people, and the resources required. Always ask for early warning indicators to avoid late surprises and make yourself available for consultation along the way. This will significantly reduce the perceived risk of delegating.

Any Breaking of the Boundaries Must Be Made Consciously and Depends on the Context

You need both styles in your management toolkit and must apply them situationally. Both are valid if they are consciously chosen rather than because of an unconscious, innate drive. For example, the reasons for being more directive could include a short-term lack of capacity or expertise, poor performance, an extreme deadline, a fundamental turnaround, etc. The reason for being more participative could include showing the humility to ask for others' opinions, giving learning opportunities to people with potential, knowing full well that they might fail the first time, or showing trust in someone who's previously made a mistake to uphold, rather than destroy, their momentarily fragile self-esteem, etc.

In the Long Run, the Participative Style Is Far Superior to the Directive Style

When a leader has no intrinsic control issues and their team is made up of A-players, the participative approach is clearly far superior to the directive approach. It allows leaders to tap deeper into the capabilities and creativity of the whole team and to open many more possibilities than would otherwise be available under the directive approach, where there are fewer A-players. Delegating ownership is critical for value creation, even if it leads to some cost duplication, as we have pointed out previously. In addition, the authoritarian style of management has only two effective motivation tools – reward and punishment – whereas the motivation toolset available for the participative leader is much broader.

Actions

There are a number of actions that could be considered:

1. Practice Self-Observation. We all come with our innate biases. We are not asking you to eradicate them to become a good leader. Good leaders learn first to identify and then to live with their biases while not letting the worst take over. One way to do this is to practice self-observation. The awareness of why you're seeking control or looking for approval is an important input into the process. Yet, even if you can't get to the bottom of 'why', you can always stop these unconscious behaviours once you detect them through self-observation.

2. Surround Yourself with A-Players. A-players do not let themselves be influenced either by control issues or by a desire to be universally liked. They are well-rounded managers who can both consult and direct as the situation dictates but have no intrinsic need to orchestrate the actions and behaviours of others to compensate for their own fears. This is another reason why you need to surround yourself with A-players to improve the performance of your team.

Even then, A-players need to be directed at times in specific areas where they lack enough experience or expertise (in particular, for items on the Management Agenda). That's why if you, as a people manager or a CEO, have more experience than your team members, which is highly likely, you should always remain flexible in your approach to management. Given the specific situation, you can be as directive as you want, but the key is not to let the authoritarian approach become endemic in your organisation.

Potential Pitfalls

Authoritarian tendencies are often associated with an unrelenting focus on the Value Goal, extreme drive to succeed, and seeking unrealistic results, etc. Despite the positive outcomes, if these tendencies remain unconscious and unrecognised, they could be detrimental to any organisation in the long term.

In addition, such positive outcomes are usually the result of the high personal capabilities of authoritarian individuals rather than their management style. It must be remembered that correlation does not equal causation.

We should also not forget that in the long run, the authoritarian approach is always more limiting because it relies on the capabilities and the creativity of only one (or very few trusted people) rather than the team (or the organisation) as a whole.

25. Crisis Management: How to Manage Effectively in a Crisis

Issue: A crisis requires a distinctively different leadership approach than business as usual.

Now and then in the life of every company, there is a crisis. It does not matter who the CEO is, what its Management Model is, what markets it operates in, or what its history is. It is just a matter of probabilities – sooner or later, every company will stumble at the tail-end of the probability distribution curve.

A crisis happens when the company's survival or independence is put on the line. It can arise swiftly, or it can be a long time coming. In all cases, when it occurs, it breaks down all corporate routines. It cannot be dealt with through the normal Operating Rhythm and decision-making process. It demands a new, discrete set of principles, processes, and decision-making rules to overcome the crisis and minimise the potential damage.

Crises can be classified into a set number of categories:

- Acts of nature, e.g., natural disasters, deadly pandemics, etc.
- Acts of people, e.g., data breaches, armed conflicts, kidnapping, hacking, etc.
- Acts of macro-economics, e.g., the global financial crisis of 2008, run-on bank deposits, etc.
- Acts of Idiosyncrasy, e.g., misconduct, Regulator punishment, hostile takeover bid, etc.

Even though most of the above examples might appear like completely random events, the fact is that a tail event should be contemplated and planned for, even if the detail remains unknown.

Very often, one type of crisis causes a shockwave of spill-over effects that might take years to recover. For example, following the global financial crisis of 2008, the Irish banking sector collapsed at the start of 2009. The Irish State, the European Central Bank, the International Monetary Fund and the European Commission had to intervene to save the sector. The banks that survived the initial shock then entered a series of knock-on crises which continued for the next ten years. These included: the preparation of restructuring plans, bad debt management, portfolio fire sales, misconduct scandals, regulatory fines, potential run-on deposits, etc. Many of the affected banks had to apply the principles of crisis management described below to cope with the changing situation for years following the original economic shock.

Principles

Extreme Realism

When the company's survival is on the line, leadership must face up to the hard facts so they can meet the crisis head-on. An evaluation of the situation must be done quickly and resolutely. Hiring an independent external adviser to do this objectively can also be a good idea.

It does not matter if the facts are painful or if they paint the key decision-makers in a bad light. It also does not matter what caused the crisis in the first place. There will be plenty of time to analyse the causes when it is over. Dealing with the raw and extreme reality is the only way to get through to the other side.

Complete Alignment

From the very beginning, leadership must ensure complete alignment across the organisation towards the common cause of survival. This means two things. First, everyone should be on the same page about the fact surrounding the crisis. And second, everyone should be clear about their specific responsibilities in terms of handling it.

Panic Mitigation

If unchecked, there is always a risk of panic spreading among company employees, customers, the press, or the public at large. Succumbing to this panic must be avoided at all costs as it will interfere with the ability of the organisation to contain the crisis. Transparency (i.e., telling the truth) and visibility of leadership are key to preventing panic.

Asset Protection

Certain types of crises require fast reactions to protect existing company assets. Examples include data breaches, hacking, or bad sales practices, all of which must be stopped quickly. Effective asset protection requires a factual assessment of the situation and quick involvement of legal advisers.

Lightspeed Decision-Making and Execution

Time is a luxury in a crisis. The decision-making process and speed of execution must be accelerated to an extreme. This often means concentrating decision-making and execution power on a small number of individuals, such as a 'crisis management team'. It also means immediate activation of any relevant crisis management action plans or protocols, which must be executed at pace. Having planned for a crisis in advance can sometimes make all the difference between survival and liquidation.

Laser-Like Focus

A crisis, by definition, creates a multitude of issues. It is the Board's and CEO's responsibility to have the courage to focus on what really matters to protect the franchise. This capability requires choice, saying 'no', upsetting the 'apple cart', and a bias towards a directive style of leadership.

Actions

Assess Quickly the Situation

A quick and level-headed assessment of the situation is the priority of leadership. They need to address the following questions:

5

5

- What are the facts as we currently understand them, acknowledging that these may change as the crisis develops?
- How much time do we have before the point of no return?
- What is the worst-case scenario and its consequences?
- What is the human and financial cost that we are likely to suffer?
- What really matters in terms of franchise protection?

It is critical that the assessment follows the principles above so that the crisis can be met head-on.

Summon a Crisis Management Team

It is perfectly acceptable to adopt a more authoritarian management style during a crisis. Decision-making power, communications, and execution should be concentrated to increase reaction speed and mitigate panic.

Appoint a cross-functional team led by one Accountable Executive. At a minimum, the crisis management team should include the key decision-makers in the organisation (such as the COO and CTO, etc.) as well as a communications expert, a legal adviser, and, if required, representatives of colleagues and/or customers. It is imperative to appoint your most experienced people to the crisis management team. Different categories of crises might require different decision-makers on the crisis management team.

Activate Existing Crisis Plans

Even though most crises cannot be foreseen with certainty, companies can, without a doubt, have a plan for many of them. Therefore, the first decision of the crisis management team must be to activate the existing crisis plan (such as the Business Continuity Plan, the Business Recovery Plan, etc.) depending on the issue at hand. This is where advanced disaster planning is critical, as it will significantly accelerate the company's reaction time and risk mitigation activities.

If no plan exists (and this should be an extremely rare occasion), the crisis management team must formulate a plan as soon as possible based on the situation assessment. Having to iterate the plan based on a new set of facts should not be a cause for panic, as many companies found out during the COVID-19 pandemic. For example, COVID's advent caused all banks to adopt a new operating model – including a new customer service model, staff working model, and risk management model – virtually overnight. In the space of a very short period, ways of working changed fundamentally. This change was executed at speed, and interestingly, value was created as new approaches were designed and implemented. A key learning was the adaptivity of A-players and their ability to take calculated risks.

Communicate Directly to Contain Panic

Regular communications, both internal and external, are extremely important during a crisis. There is nothing worse than radio silence during an unfolding crisis. People always tend to assume the worst, and lack of communication is inevitably going to lead to wide-spread rumours, fear, and panic.

Being transparent with the truth and being visible to everyone affected are the two most important elements of good communication. It is not advisable to conceal any facts, as the truth will always come out in the end. Communications must also include both the content of the plan to resolve the crisis and the process itself. In other words, leadership must announce that they have a plan, explain what the plan is, and then provide frequent updates about how the execution of the plan is going.

In any case, communications must always show empathy for affected groups of people. Only then will communication take care of both the emotional and the rational needs of people and open an opportunity for leadership to ask colleagues to align behind the plan and help with its execution.

Protect Existing Assets

Following a quick assessment of the situation, leadership must move in quickly to protect any key assets from lasting damage. For example, any bad practices must be stopped immediately, and any potential spill-over effect must be evaluated and addressed at pace. Legal advisers must be engaged and appointed to the crisis management team.

Create a Management Agenda

The creation of a Management Agenda to highlight the highest franchise protection issues and opportunities is key. All stakeholders must align behind what really matters in a crisis and have the courage to say 'no'. This will mean the alienation of certain key stakeholders, the allocation of resources to only a select number of initiatives, the potential loss of talented resources, and, potentially, long-lasting damage to relationships. Unfortunately, this can be the price of survival. Resilience, focus, and courage are the leadership traits required.

Potential Pitfalls

Denial and wishful thinking must be avoided at all costs. Consider the worst and be prepared to respond on that basis if necessary.

Poor communication, lack of transparency, and lack of leadership visibility are very detrimental in times of crisis. One cannot afford to underestimate the importance of internal and external communications.

Furthermore, managing a crisis using a business-as-usual approach is a grave mistake. It is also true that one cannot manage a company in a perennial crisis mode for a long time. In addition to wearing people down quickly, it is very expensive and unsustainable in the long run, although it could be very tempting for leaders with authoritarian tendencies (see Chapter 28).

Once the crisis has been managed to resolution, complete a review to identify the root cause and put in place policies and procedures to mitigate any recurrence.

26. Silent Disagreement: How to Deal with It Effectively

Issue: At C-suite level, any covert or silent disagreement with the Governing Objective, Vision, or Management Model can create significant problems for the CEO.

Disagreement is not something to be shunned in business. Far from it. It should give rise to a discussion which is healthy by nature. Following the principles of good decision-making outlined in Chapter 6, fact-based and alternative-driven discussions should, in principle, lead to better decisions.

The problem arises when a leader is faced with covert or, as we would like to call it, 'silent' disagreement with the key foundations underpinning their Management Model. This will often happen in companies where people are afraid of speaking up and expressing views openly due to the specificity of the culture or due to previous incidents where a colleague was punished for expressing their views openly. It could also be due to prior conditioning (i.e., jobs in other companies) or if the prevalent management style is somewhat intimidating.

In addition, silent disagreement can happen if the selection and recruitment process does not present a clear view of the Governing Objective, Vision, and Management Model to candidates or if the interview process does not weed out those who hold alternative (if misguided) views about business. Of course, this does not mean that we are advocating 'groupthink' – we think it is the role of the leader to encourage diversity of thought to deliver the

Governing Objective within the boundaries of the Vision and Management Model.

The problem is that silent disagreement often leads to various passive-aggressive behaviours, such as gossiping, disengagement, aloofness, disconnection, procrastination, avoidance, as well as the pursuit of pet projects. Such behaviours have the potential not only to poison the culture of any organisation but also to sabotage even the best strategies and CEOs. No good leader can afford such behaviours under their watch as it distracts from the spirit of 'team' and, critically, the discretionary effort that this spirit generates. Of course, leaders must show awareness by reflecting on their own management style and question whether it could be a driver for silence around the table – and respond if that is the case.

For example, due to under-performance, the Board brings in a new CEO from the outside. They have very clear and vocal ideas about how the company should be managed and what the new strategy should be. Some incumbent executives are quite naturally scared for their jobs and choose to disagree silently without voicing a challenge, despite having plenty of opportunities to do so. At the same time, the CEO is so occupied with the new strategy that they fail to notice an emerging problem. Despite the improvement in corporate performance in the short term, in the long run, this results in a lot of mutual frustration and misunderstanding, in addition to wasting a lot of valuable resources and time.

Principles

There are a number of principles that must be applied:

1. Ensure the team is wholly aligned behind the Blueprint. The CEO cannot afford to be any silent disagreement from ExCo. Therefore, alignment should occur at the earliest possible moment, which is during the selection and recruitment process of the top team. The CEO should spend enough time during this process to test for alignment with the intended 'ways of working', e.g., if the candidates align with the Governing Objective. The skill is to find a diverse team in terms of, for example, gender, race, and age that aligns around the core beliefs but provides a diversity of thought.

The CEO should also apply the same rigour for incumbents. In simple terms, lack of alignment should mean a dignified exit. For those who 'escape the net', the CEO must have the courage to recognise misalignment and exit those executives with grace and dignity. To be clear, we are arguing that there is a huge difference between 'silent disagreement' (and fundamental misalignment) and having diversity of thought and opinion within the Blueprint framework. The two are not the same, as one of the authors (Jeremy) has found to a high cost over the course of a career – 'silent disagreement' is one of the great energy-sappers for a CEO.

2. Divide all important corporate decisions into three broad categories: (i) ways of working decisions, (ii) strategic decisions, and (iii) tactical decisions, and get alignment on them in that order.

Ways of working decisions pertain to how an organisation is to be managed. They usually fall in the decision domain of the CEO (subject to agreement by the Board) and include areas such as establishing a Governing Objective, setting the Vision, embedding the Management Model, and developing the right Corporate Culture.

Strategic decisions pertain to what markets the company chooses to compete in and how it chooses to compete in those markets. They usually fall in the decision domain of the ExCo and again are subject to the agreement by the Board. They include approval of medium-term Strategic and Financial Plans, resource allocation, approval of next year's budget, etc. Alignment around the strategic decisions should take place during the annual IPP. The process itself should include several specific juncture points, where executives should feel encouraged to voice disagreement and engage in discussion with the CEO, CFO, other executives, and the Board. We are used to calling these points 'Strategic and Financial Dialogues' to signify the discussions that need to take place. The Board should act as an arbiter in those cases where the differences seem irreconcilable. A good example of how misalignment can happen is if the CEO is managing for value and the CFO is managing market metrics and short-term optics or key members of the ExCo misunderstand the notion of Customer Value. Again, always find executives who are aligned in mind and spirit around the core beliefs.

Tactical decisions define the concrete steps to execute the strategy as well as the whole host of daily decisions required to run the company. They usually fall in the decision domain of specific executives and sometimes might require ExCo approval if there are critical interdependencies between the areas of accountability of different executives. They include things like Execution Plans, project budgets, timelines, deliverables, etc. Even though tactical decisions are a prerogative of the individual executives, they too cannot afford silent disagreement in any areas where they depend on other executives. Unsurprisingly this covers a whole host of important decisions. The forum for seeking alignment around such decisions is the ExCo meetings. The CEO should act as an arbiter in those cases where the differences seem irreconcilable.

3. Make sure that your own management style is not the culprit. Of course, none of the above matters too much if the management style of the CEO or some of the executives is intimidating or overly dominating. If you are this person, make sure that you read the chapters on style and behaviours in the workplace and reflect. You need to be clear about your own management style – why and where you choose to use an authoritarian or participative style – bearing in mind that an excessive authoritarian style will always breed a lot of silent disagreement and passive-aggressive behaviour. Nothing good will come out of intimidation and domination in the long run. Your task is exactly the opposite to avoid silent disagreement. You must maintain an environment of psychological safety. That said, 'standing for something' in terms of a clear approach (in our case, Governing Objective, Vision, and Management Model) does allow candidates or existing executives the choice of whether to be part of the CEO's team.

Actions

There are a number of actions that could be considered:

1. Management Model Decisions. Any candidate or incumbent must demonstrate alignment with the Governing Objective, Vision, and Management Model envisioned by the CEO during the selection and recruitment process. This is how the CEO will create alignment from the onset.

The most important element here is alignment with the Governing Objective. Of course, as we have said previously, the skill is to balance the 'non-negotiables' with the power of 'co-creation' – a difficult balance but one worth the time and effort.

2. Strategic Decisions. The IPP should be designed with the aim of achieving alignment around the strategic decisions facing the company. A very important part of this is applying the principles of the Management Agenda, as this will also ensure proper prioritisation of the dialogues around the executive table. Another element of achieving alignment around the strategic decision is the application of proper decision-making standards (Factbase, Alternatives, and Decision Rules).

3. Tactical Decisions. Create the conditions of psychological safety to encourage quality conversations by enforcing the boundaries of the Management Model and, at the same time, allowing people to check and challenge each other.

Potential Pitfalls

Sometimes silent disagreement and the related passive-aggressive behaviours are a result of past conditioning (i.e., another job) and are a foundational part of how people perceive the world. Other times, it is based on ego and intellectual arrogance. It would take a lot of time and patience to overcome such conditioning.

Below are some examples of where silent disagreement arises most frequently in our experience:

- The validity of the Governing Objective – there are always going to be people who do not align with the idea that maximising the value for the company's owners should be the Governing Objective.
- The focus on value through the Management Agenda – there are always going to be 'busy fools' who are motivated by feeling busy and who cannot align behind the discipline of focus based on value-at-stake.
- The focus on value-based versus market-based measures when discussing performance – there are always those whose intellectual frame of reference is shaped by market measures and who will not align

behind the fundamentals of intrinsic value management and its core beliefs (including that market measures are for relative performance comparisons and are an outturn of great value-based management).

- The positioning of the customer – there are always going to be people who are going to proclaim all customers are equally important to the company and that 'customer centricity' is the Governing Objective. Of course, not all customers are equal, valuable, or loyal. What is important is to understand customer economics first, then design products which distinguish you from the competition.

- The power of facts – anywhere that factbase insights contradict people's entrenched ideas about the business, the market, or the customer causes friction. Therefore, the importance of a robust factbase must always take precedence over gutfeel or previous experience (that must be respected as a controlling factor before any final decision is made). For example, it is important to understand where value is created first and then act on this knowledge, rather than following the clichéd wisdom of taking care of your customers and employees first and then hoping for good things to happen on their own. This is essentially gambling with the owners' money.

Finally, note that there is a category of people who, no matter what you do, will never take the chance to express disagreement openly and will not support your decisions with their actions. Eventually, they need to be managed out without regret.

27. Stress: How to Recognise and Deal with It Effectively

Issue: Excessive stress can lead to a deterioration in one's productivity, creativity, and health and impact those around you.

We were unsure whether to include this chapter in the book. We have no medical qualifications and do not purport to be experts in the field. As such, we hope the reader allows us to enter the space in good faith and provide some of our own experiences and observations.

Excessive stress has become pervasive in the modern world. Everyone is under pressure to perform better, produce more, move faster, react quicker, and think deeper. This may well be manageable if it applied just to our professional lives, but that's not the case. The pressure applies to all aspects of our lives and is driven, in large part, by the information overload that accompanies an 'always on' culture.

It should be noted that not all stress is harmful. Up to a certain point of tolerance it can be beneficial as it helps people sharpen their attention and improve reactions. It depends on the individual where exactly this point is, but beyond it, stress is harmful.

Principles

There are a number of principles that must be applied:

1. Dealing with stress is strictly personal. In addition to having different levels of stress tolerance, sources of stress can differ for different people. What makes one person stressed may not bother another and the other way around.

Leading Without Winging It

The leader may be able to manage the work environment and any major sources of stress, but they cannot manage how individual team members deal with it. Therefore, it is up to the leader to set the right conditions of psychological safety.

What others will do depends to a large extent on their self-awareness. This self-awareness drives their resilience. People with lower self-awareness react completely automatically to stress (see the four stress-coping mechanisms below) and often exhibit feelings of victimhood and helplessness in the face of stressful events.

People with higher self-awareness tend to know or are at least interested in finding out what the causes of stress. They ask themselves:

- What are the thoughts and the emotions that trigger my stress?
- What are my reactions in stressful situations?
- Do my reactions repeat themselves in different situations?

It is important to note that the thoughts and emotions that trigger stress are not readily apparent to external observers. That said, behavioural reactions to stress are apparent to external observers if they know what to look for. Things like displays of anger or stupor, engaging in too many activities, and overeating or drinking are oftentimes obvious and might signify specific stress-coping mechanisms at play.

2. There are four stress-coping mechanisms (Fight, Flight, Freeze, and Fawn), collectively known as the '4Fs'. Being aware of these four strategies is very important both from the individual point of view, i.e., for increasing your own self-awareness, and from the leader's point of view, i.e., for setting the right conditions of psychological safety in your team.

It is important to understand that everyone, without exception, learns these strategies by trial and error as a child. Based on their relative success, one takes up a preference for one or two of these strategies as being more reliable than the others. What one chooses to prefer is, more or less, a random function of environmental variables such as the behaviours of their parents, siblings, friends, the school environment, and anything else that can influence a young person's mind. These one or two preferred strategies then become their dominant ways of dealing with stress as an adult.

All in all, the point is that we can learn to spot how we and others react to stress, which is valuable information for dealing with it effectively.

Fight

'Fight' is a stress-coping defence mechanism that is principally characterised by excessive focus on self and lack of empathy for others. When faced with a perceived threat from others, people who use 'Fight' as a stress-coping strategy are ready to attack with disregard for others. It does not matter if the threat is real or imaginary; their primary concern is their own survival, regardless of the potential casualties. 'Fight' is also known as the 'narcissistic defence'.

The positive or healthy sides of 'Fight' include strong personal boundaries, assertive nature, knowing what you want, and being perceived externally as a strong person (even though internally you might be feeling weak). The negative or unhealthy sides of 'Fight' include the inability to maintain meaningful relationships in and out of the workplace, visible displays of anger, and perceiving oneself as weak or even incompetent, despite the outward displays of strength.

At work, these are usually the people who always want to be the centre of attention, who are always ready to jump at you, bully others, or pursue their own egoistical goals with disregard for the well-being of others or the company itself. As your boss, they will push you to the limit, especially if you don't have healthy personal boundaries yourself (see the 'Fawn' mechanism below).

Flight (Escape)

'Flight' is a stress-coping defence mechanism characterised by either removing oneself from the threatening situation or, when this is not often possible, removing one's attention to more pleasurable activities or thoughts. It is also known as the 'obsessive-compulsive defence' because the automatic thoughts or activities temporality relieve the experience of stress. Employing this stress defence often means escaping into day-dreams full of perfection, order, and harmony (e.g., imagining the perfect relationship, the perfect job, the perfect boss, etc) where, unlike the real world, the lack of these attributes is a major cause of stress.

The positive or healthy sides of 'Flight' include having very high standards of oneself and others, having deep expert knowledge in one or numerous subjects (which they accumulated during their escape missions in these subjects), and very often being a workaholic (work as a means of an escape by activity). The negative or unhealthy sides of 'Flight' include constant disappointment with oneself or others (for having not met their own high standards), strong resistance to people, behaviours, and events that do not fit into their expectations of order and perfection, and, most importantly, almost constant fatigue because they are spending so much energy on maintaining their escape activities and thoughts.

At work, these are usually some of your best employees – hard-working experts who are always on the look-out for problems to fix. Unfortunately, they often pay the price of complete exhaustion. They will always be more knowledgeable and more capable than you and will always find faults with your work, which might be discouraging at times.

Freeze

'Freeze' is a stress-coping defence mechanism characterised by dissociation. It often clicks in when stress is so overwhelming that the only thing one can do is to switch off completely one's attention. This is often associated with food (especially copious amounts of sugar), alcohol, and even drugs. Also, if a perceived threat is very intense and surprising (say someone is very aggressive to you during a meeting in the office), 'Freeze' can also show up as a stupor or lapse of clear thinking. Oftentimes after such an event, you think to yourself, 'Why didn't I say this or that? Why didn't it occur to me?' Well, the answer is that your mind froze. 'Freeze' is also known as the 'dissociative defence'.

People with a dominant tendency to freeze in the face of perceived threats usually prefer to work on their own and could be very good at solitary activities such as programming or single-player sports, such as chess. These activities are the positive or healthy sides of 'Freeze'. The negative or unhealthy sides of 'Freeze' include giving the impression of being incapable or poor at what they are supposed to do because they froze at the wrong moment.

For example, we used to know a senior executive who was always very aggressive with everyone and was known to fire people on the spot if not liking what they were saying. The behaviours and reputation were enough to put even the best people in a complete stupor when they met this individual. This 'Freeze' reaction was then interpreted as a lack of capability, which led to more unjustified dismissals.

Fawn

'Fawn' is a stress defence mechanism characterised by displays of helpfulness, care, co-operation, concern, or any behaviour that signals to the perceived perpetrator, 'I am not a threat to you' or 'I'm on your side, and I'd like to help you.' People who practice 'Fawn' offer to exchange helpfulness for protection. 'Fawn' is also known as the 'co-dependency defence'.

The positive or healthy sides of 'Fawn' include being helpful and supportive to others, always willing to get fully involved in what the boss wants and being always available for extra work or any other activities. The negative or unhealthy sides of 'Fawn' include a lack of personal boundaries, inability to say 'no', neediness for positive feedback, and giving out the impression of being weak (even though internally they might be experiencing themselves as strong survivors).

At work, bosses who employ the 'Fight' mechanism often surround themselves with 'Yes' people (who employ the 'Fawn' mechanism), which is a phenomenon that can bring serious issues for the organisation.

3. Being an A-player has nothing to do with your preferred stress-coping defences. How people react automatically to stress has nothing to do with whether they are an A-player or not. What makes an A-player is the ability for self-awareness and the willingness to take action, despite one's own automatic tendencies.

As mentioned, a person uses one or two dominating stress-coping defences that they learnt as a child, and which are deeply engrained in their sub-conscious. With enough self-awareness and willingness to act, these should not be problems to deal with; that is, to eliminate the negative or unhealthy side-effects described above.

The more serious problems arise for individuals and the company they are working for when these defence mechanisms are taken to extreme application; for example, when 'Fight' turns into sociopathy or 'Fawn' turns into servitude. A-player status becomes untenable if any of these happens.

Actions

We have divided potential actions into two broad categories: (i) helping oneself and (ii) helping others.

Helping Oneself

There are a number of actions in this category that must be considered:

1. Practice self-awareness. We already mentioned that lower levels of self-awareness tend to sustain and reinforce the automatic stress-coping mechanisms that people have adopted since childhood. Therefore, working consciously towards heightened self-awareness should improve one's resilience to stress.

There are two areas for improved self-awareness: physical and mental. In terms of physical awareness, one should make a conscious effort to become aware of the effects of stress on the body. For example, one can start with questions like this:

- Have I been gaining or losing weight due to stress? Am I eating or drinking too much?
- Are there any places in the body where pain gets activated when I am stressed?
- How am I breathing when I'm stressed?

The answers to these questions will help us become more aware of the costs. They will also help us identify and tackle stressful situations quicker than before.

In terms of mental awareness, one should focus on two key places:

- What are my key thoughts and emotions which trigger stress?
- What are my one or two preferred stress-coping mechanisms (of the 4Fs), and how do they manifest in my daily life?

The answer to these questions will allow us to see that most of the stress is self-inflicted – more of a function of one's imagination than a real threat to one's survival. The answers will also help us identify and challenge the repetitive patterns that play out every time we are stressed.

2. Stop reactivity (automatic reactions). As one's self-awareness increases, one discovers that it becomes much easier to catch oneself when stressed and maximise the space between stimulus and response. As such, at this moment, it is important to give oneself enough time and safe space to process what is going on by:

- Reframing one's stress triggers into challenges
- Taking care of one's stressed body through practicing relaxation, deeper breathing, sports, or even some nourishing food
- Taking care of one's mind through practicing meditation, listening to favourite music, reading a good book, etc.

3. Focus on one's own priorities. Feeling stressed tends to be overwhelming, especially when one of the 4Fs is triggered automatically. In such moments, it is important to remember one's own personal priorities (see Chapter 16) and re-focus our attention on them. This will give us a perspective and increase our resilience by recollecting what is most important in our lives.

Helping Others

There is another set of actions in this category that must be considered:

1. Provide safe space and sufficient time. Dealing with stress requires time and a safe space. Therefore, creating and maintaining an environment of psychological safety is very important. When you discover that a member of your team has gone beyond their stress tolerance point and is acting out one of the 4Fs mechanisms, we suggest the first thing that you need to do is to give time and space to alleviate the stress.

2. Suspend judgement. In all cases, we suggest you suspend judgement. Remember, all four stress-coping mechanisms are just like software programmes running in the sub-conscious. When they play out, a person's ability to take corrective actions is at its lowest.

However, we think you can judge a person's capacity for self-awareness and their willingness to act on it. As we mentioned before, this is what distinguishes the A-player from everyone else.

3. Trigger self-awareness with the right questions. When you observe the application of specific stress-coping defences by members of your team, we suggest you can help improve self-awareness by asking some well-crafted questions. In the case of:

- 'Fight' – ask them to think about the impact of their behaviours on others; how do the others around them feel; how can they take care of others better?
- 'Flight' – ask them why they are spreading themselves so thin across multiple activities or why they are so fatigued; give them assurance that they are doing good work; send them home if working long hours'; agree a focussed Management Agenda.
- 'Freeze' – check in regularly; ask them directly for their concerns and assure them that there is nothing to worry about; if needed, reassign them to another project where their stress triggers will be less sensitive.
- 'Fawn' – ask about their own opinions before you disclose yours; explain that you expect them to challenge you and their colleagues if they disagree without fear of retribution.

4. Provide resilience training. Finally, you can supplement all the above with some training on topics like resilience, time management, energy management, and personal priority management.

Potential Pitfalls

The automatism of the 4Fs is deeply ingrained in all of us. No one can expect to deal with their stress-coping mechanisms quickly. Sometimes the triggers are buried so deep in the sub-conscious that there is no realistic hope of getting to them. This does not mean that one cannot work on minimising the negative side-effects when they show up.

28. Narcissistic Behaviours: How to Deal with Them Effectively

Issue: If allowed to flourish, narcissistic behaviours can be very destructive in the workplace.

Everyone who has spent some time in the corporate world knows people with these characteristics: driven, focused on their personal agenda, and ready to remove all obstacles in their way. These people often reach the highest levels of the corporate hierarchy. The question is whether they are very ambitious and talented or whether they are shamelessly self-serving and ready to destroy everything in their path. Sometimes it's hard to tell the difference.

What distinguishes the 'corporate narcissists' from the talented and results-driven managers is the fundamental disregard for others. This is often accompanied by the belief that internal rules and regulations do not apply to them. This means that 'corporate narcissists' will steamroll everyone and everything on their way to deliver their own agenda, regardless of the consequences for others or for the company they work for.

In the article, 'The Psychopath in the C-Suite', INSEAD professor Manfred Kets de Vries defines a type of personality that called on SOB, short for Seductive Operational Bully: 'SOBs can be found wherever power, status, or money is at stake,' the author wrote. 'Outwardly normal, apparently successful and charming, their inner lack of empathy, shame, guilt, or remorse, has serious interpersonal repercussions, and can destroy organisations.'[18]

Having people like these in any organisation is ultimately very costly, even though their presence could be initially masked by great short-term results. Moreover, if narcissistic behaviours are tolerated by management, people can start seeing the narcissist as a role model. This way, over time, everyone who is ambitious might decide to adopt these behaviours. As a result, the behaviours spread like poison ivy and turn the organisation into a toxic pit.

You can find SOBs in almost every industry:

- The talented dealers who don't mind insider trading or price fixing because it serves them, even though it's against the law.
- The powerful CEOs who care more about their celebrity status than the people they lead.
- The corporate executives who think society's rules don't apply to them.
- The slick managers who fawn over their superiors while behaving despicably with the people in their own team.
- The managers who blame others for their mistakes but never have the courage to look at themselves.
- The managers who shamelessly take credit for the work of others.

The list goes on…

Principles

There are a number of key principles that must be applied:

Definition

The key personality trait which strongly suggests the presence of narcissistic tendencies is the complete lack of empathy.[19] Lack of empathy is defined as the inability to understand how other people feel or the lack of interest therein.

---

[18] M.F.R. Kets de Vries, 'The Psychopath in the C-Suite: Redefining the SOB', *INSEAD Faculty and Research Working Paper*, 2012.

[19] We avoid using the term 'narcissism' because it has very specific definition in psychology and calling someone a 'narcissist' can imply a diagnosis of a psychological disorder. This is not what we are talking about in this chapter.

In daily behaviour, this inability shows up as arrogance, inflated self-importance, and an unhealthy need to be admired. It also results in an inability to enter meaningful relationships with others. For such people, all relationships – both personal and professional – are transactional; that is, there must be an exchange between the parties, and the outcome is always (without exception) defined as win/lose. Therefore, they like to tread over others with no empathy in the pursuit of their own agenda and often disregard norms, regulations, and laws. As a matter of fact, people with narcissistic tendencies despise norms, regulations, and laws because they are often seen as a barrier to winning ruthlessly.

We must emphasise that being very ambitious and focused on the Value Goal is possible without being self-centred and arrogant. As a matter of fact, being ambitious and being able to relate to others at the same time is a very important component of being an A-player at work.

Cost

The long-term cost of narcissistic behaviours in the workplace is always higher than short-term gains. As we pointed out previously, in the long run, the strategy of co-operation between colleagues is always superior to the strategy of cut-throat competition as it relies on the talents, the knowledge, and the capabilities of many people instead of just one – no matter how capable they are.

The long-term cost of such behaviours include:
- Alienation of team members
- Unworkable or broken relationships with colleagues, customers, Regulators, and the community
- Reputational damage
- Deals which are bad for the company but have personal benefit

There is also a wide-spread belief in the corporate world that CEOs need to be somewhat narcissistic to be effective in their work. In our opinion, this belief is false. A CEO who cannot understand how the people feel around them, who cannot form win-win relationships with their colleagues, who seeks admiration or domination, and whose personal interest always comes before the interests of the company, cannot ever be an effective leader.

Actions
There are a number of actions that could be considered:

Job Candidates
With the above principles in mind, it is important to screen for SOBs during the selection and recruitment process. Using the 'WHO' technique described earlier in the book, the interviewer must be on the look-out for some of the following giveaways (via Prof. Kets de Vries):

- Does the person come across as too glib and too charming?
- Are they very self-centred?
- Do they enjoy being the centre of attention?
- Are they lacking in empathy?
- Are they lying convincingly?
- Does the person fawn over more senior executives with little recognition of, or respect for, more junior staff?
- Do they seek public glorification?

'If the answer is yes to more than a few such questions – and the list goes on – then the chances are,' says Prof. Kets de Vries, 'that you are dealing with an SOB.'

Although the above can be observed at any time during the selection process, the best place to test for it is during the cultural fit interview and then to double-check your suspicions during the detailed reference checks.

Incumbent Employees
It is relatively more difficult to deal with SOBs if they are on the company's payroll because they could be producing good results already, and the cost of their behaviours might not be that obvious – yet. The key in such cases is to maintain a team or Corporate Culture where the cost of such behaviours cannot go unnoticed. Below are some of the things that you can do:

- Maintain an environment of psychological safety. If someone feels that they are being bullied or if they witness other disturbing behaviours, they must feel free to speak up.
- Enforce strict accountability for one's actions. If someone's behaviour conflicts with the Governing Objective, the Vision, or the Management Model, then there must be consequences.
- Do not ignore someone's disregard for others because you or your team rely on the results that they bring in. If you ignore such behaviour (or, God forbid, you reward it), others will immediately imitate it, and narcissistic behaviours will spread.
- Encourage teamwork and sharing. As SOBs do not like to co-operate with others, this might even get them to leave the company on their own accord.
- Demand to see the alternatives in decision-making. SOBs don't like to make decisions based on alternatives because, in their minds, they are always right, and they want to impose their own solution.
- Look out for talented people leaving the company who have been driven away by bullying or behaviours from others that you might not be aware of.

Your Boss

Finally, if your boss or the CEO of your company display narcissistic behaviours, our advice is not to take them on, as you're unlikely to come out with healthy self-esteem. The best strategy, in the long run, is always to move on.

Potential Pitfalls

There are a number of pitfalls that one must be aware of and manage carefully:

1. SOBs are often very capable, talented, and results-driven individuals. Thus, recognising their cost to the company is not always easy and could require short-term sacrifices. Even if you recognise the cost of SOBs, it is often too tempting to close your eyes. Don't let that happen, as you will certainly regret that later.

2. SOBs are often very seductive. If they want, they can make anyone feel uniquely special in their presence. Senior managers, CEOs, and even Board members are not inoculated against the human need to feel important. Hence, SOBs are often tolerated and even encouraged by these senior people. 'They can't be that bad towards their staff. Look at the great behaviours with me' – is often what they tell themselves. Again, you will live to regret this mistake.

3. Finally, Boards and CEOs must rely on their own managerial intuition to mitigate the corporate narcissists. But what happens if the CEO or the Board members are the culprits themselves? Well, the shareholders will most certainly foot the bill.

29. Interpersonal Rivalry: How to Deal with It Effectively

Issue: When interpersonal rivalry gets out of hand, it can prove destructive for high-performing teams.

It is in our human nature to judge, compare, and compete. Often, we compare ourselves to an ideal or high standard, and at other times, we compare ourselves to others. In a work context, such comparisons are inevitable and often lead to rivalry. Even though competition is healthy to a certain extent as it pushes people to improve, it can also be destructive.

Destructive rivalry takes place when people are no longer working towards a common aspiration, such as the company's Governing Objective and Vision but instead start pursuing their own agenda at the expense of colleagues and the company itself. Such rivalry can lead to some very negative consequences for any team with a significant cost attached, such as:

- Inferior decision-making
- Spoilt relationships
- Poor communication
- Procrastination
- Gossiping, etc...

Destructive rivalry is usually motivated by ego or narcissistic tendencies, which are toxic to high-performing teams, as we describe in Chapter 28. In addition, any overt or tacit encouragement of unhealthy rivalry will signal to everyone on the team that such behaviour is okay, and this can lead to a vicious downward spiral.

For example, two people might be involved in an unhealthy rivalry situation. They are both very ambitious and want their boss to like them, but their means are different. One is aggressive and dominant in their interactions with others, while the other is a quiet perfectionist and a people-pleaser. While caught up in an intense rivalry, both are trying to convince their boss that they are better than the other without communicating and interacting with each other. This is a good example of what we call a 'triangle' relationship, where two people communicate through a third person, usually their boss, but not to each other. Even though they are both individually producing good work, there is no synergy.

In another example three of the directors of a company compete intensely with each other, resulting in a similar type of 'triangle' relationship with the CEO – recognising that the math doesn't work here, but you'll understand what we mean. The difference is that, in this case, the future success of the company is predicated on the effectiveness of co-operation and communication. Not only is there no synergy between the three, but also their competitive relationship will destroy enormous value for the company.

Both examples show that in the presence of unhealthy rivalry, the sum of the parts is less than the whole.

Principles

There are a number of principles that must be applied:

1. There is a boundary between creative competition and destructive rivalry. Diversity of thinking always enhances the quality of management decisions so long as a proper decision-making process is followed. We described this process in a fair amount of detail in Chapter 6 (Factbase, Alternatives, and Decision Rules). Competition is allowed and encouraged within the process – that is, everyone should be welcome to argue about Facts, Alternatives, and Decision Rules – and discouraged outside of the process. Competition amongst your team members is inevitable, but it should not be allowed to turn into unhealthy rivalry.

2. The role of the leader is to maintain effective boundaries. They can do this by (i) ensuring that everyone understands how decisions are made and (ii)

providing feedback immediately using Radical Candor™ (as described in Chapter 22) as and when it is required (always avoiding the 'triangle'). In addition, it is very important to provide development opportunities for all team members based on a fair assessment of their needs and capabilities so that the integrity of 'enabling everyone to be the best they can be' is maintained. This way no one should feel that they have been treated unfairly or left behind for any reason. This should be your clear intent as a leader, and you must be unambiguous with your team members about it.

3. Structure and decision rights can be either a hindrance or a source of value creation. It is imperative that the leader thinks carefully about structure and associated decision rights as a means of value creation (or destruction). Even if there is a logical and rational design, it might be that it is not operationally effective. Some examples of where logic might not meet effectiveness include 'matrix'; 'dual-solid'; 'manufacturing v distribution'; 'customer v channel'. We cannot emphasise how critical it is to ensure the recruitment and selection process confirms that candidates will fit with the underlying behaviours required for a structure (that supports a strategy) to work – or iterate the structure without compromising the strategy.

Actions

There are a number of actions that could be considered:

Ways Of Working

Implementing clear and unambiguous ways of working lays the conditions for avoiding interpersonal rivalry in your company:

- Establishing a Governing Objective and Vision gives your colleagues a common purpose.
- Codifying Values and Behaviours within the Vision sets the standards for working together.
- Establishing a formal Management Model provides the boundary between creative competition and destructive rivalry between colleagues, grounded in the achievement of the Value Goal.

Performance Management and Professional Development

The role of performance management is to ensure effective enforcement of the Governing Objective, Vision, and Management Model, combined with genuine care for the individual. To that end, as a leader you should:

- Set clear scorecards for everyone on your team so there is no doubt about what is expected. Those scorecards must specifically include co-operation with fellow team members and working towards common aspirations.
- Carry out regular formal performance reviews and career conversations, which will 'take the sting' out of interpersonal rivalry as individuals see that they are treated as an investment by their boss and not as an expendable resource.
- Call out 'triangle' relationships as soon as you become aware of them and ask those involved to resolve their difference directly and come back to you with a joint solution within the confines of the formal decision-making process, involving Factbase, Alternatives, and Decision Rules.
- Manage out quickly those who cannot work to the company's Values and Behaviours (stressing again the need to spend time upfront in recruiting and selecting those who can work within the boundaries while investing in diversity of thought).

Reward and Recognition

The role of Reward and Recognition is to ensure tangible consequences for everyone on the team. To that effect, you should:

- Set a Total Reward model that rewards both individual achievements and collaboration, using both the Intrinsic and Extrinsic elements as described in Chapter 23. Make sure the model has a bias towards collaboration.
- Follow the rule of 'public recognition and private criticism' in all cases of interpersonal rivalry.

Potential Pitfalls

Some managers enjoy watching the rivalry between team members. It gives them a sense of control and domination as well as the ability to manipulate people. Such dynamics are damaging and can bring about huge individual and organisational costs. One should never engage in such behaviour, no matter how tempting.

Other managers purposefully create unrealistic expectations for team members about potential career paths or development investments to keep people striving and happy. When such unrealistic expectations are not met, individuals will inevitably start comparing and competing with their colleagues more ardently. Thus, it is critical to manage expectations – for example, by distinguishing clearly between Rockstars and Superstars as per Chapter 22 – even if the reactions are sometimes negative.

.

30. Dismissals: How to Let People Go Without Complications

Issue: Letting someone go could be an agonising process for both sides if done inappropriately.

No matter how good the recruitment and selection process or working environment is, it is inevitable that sooner or later in your career, you will have to lay someone off due to consistent under-performance or poor behaviour. Likewise, no matter how talented and knowledgeable you are, chances are that at least once in your career, you will be managed out. It's just a fact of business life.

However, many people managers feel uncomfortable letting people go for some of the following reasons:

- They empathise with the other person because they know how distressing this might be and hide behind a myriad of different reasons to avoid the truth.
- They are so innately driven to look good or to be admired that firing someone is a direct threat to this self-image.
- They don't want to admit before their own boss that they've made a mistake in hiring a particular person in the first place.

Under Kim Scott's Radical Candor™ framework, the first reason above falls under the category of Ruinous Empathy, where you personally care about others but don't dare challenge their under-performance directly.[20] The second

---

[20] Scott, *Radical Candor.*

and the third reasons above fall under the category of Manipulative Insincerity, where you neither care for the other person nor challenge their under-performance because you're too preoccupied with your own self-image.

There is also a category of managers who neither care about others nor have a problem challenging them directly. Kim Scott calls this attitude Obnoxious Aggression. They have no problem letting people go ruthlessly and even try and create a personal aura around doing so. Eventually, they create an atmosphere of fear, which in the long run can spell disaster for any organisation.

Any of the above could be a source of significant cost. This cost could manifest as:

- Your own reputational cost of being seen as unable to manage under-performance
- The opportunity cost to the organisation of not managing under-performance
- The emotional cost to the sides involved

Let's continue the example from Chapter 29 of the three directors who compete intensely with each other, thereby destroying value for the company. No matter how you look at it, destroying value is under-performance by any definition. Yet, if their boss tolerates the situation, then this can lead to several undesirable consequences. First, it damages their own reputation, as, despite talk of high performance, the boss is seen by everyone to be tolerating mediocrity. Second, the company's commercial performance takes a turn for the worse. Finally, too much valuable time and effort is spent on this issue instead of investing in the company's priorities.

Some of the perceived impediments to letting people go might include:

- 'Things are bound to get better as they spend more time with each other.'
- 'Dismissing someone will shock the others and disrupt the company.'
- 'It will be impossible to find and hire another qualified individual.'
- 'It is better to have someone in the job than an empty spot in the organisational chart.'

- 'The three of them must make it work; otherwise, I have to admit to the Board that I myself made the mistake of hiring them.'

These are examples of Ruinous Empathy accompanied by the fear of ruining one's own self-image in the process.

Principles

When it comes to letting people go, there is only one very important principle to remember.

Rational vs. Emotional Management

In situations where you consider letting someone go, it is critically important to distinguish the rational side of management (performance management) from the emotional side of management (empathy and concern for the individual). This means that you should care in equal measure both about the work (challenging under-performers directly) and the person (seeing and treating them with respect). This is what Kim Scott calls treating people with Radical Candor™.

Another way to describe this is to be dispassionate and objective about the work of your team while at the same time caring personally about each person on the team. Having an attitude of Radical Candor™ from the very beginning means that letting them go will neither be a problem for you nor for the individual.

Actions

Recruitment and Performance Management

The first step of letting people go effectively begins as early as the selection and recruitment process. Applying the principles described in Chapter 19 will significantly reduce the risk of making a hiring mistake, but it will not be eliminated. Also, people and circumstances change over time, which requires managers to remain flexible.

The second step takes place during the one-to-one Feedback and Performance Management processes. It is important to apply the principles outlined in Chapter 22, especially displaying the attitude of Radical Candor™. Everyone on your team – from the Rockstars and the Superstars to the under-performers – should know that you care about the quality of their work and care about them as people. Indeed, to care involves letting those go who are underperforming, as contradictory as that may sound.

Termination

The third and final step of letting people go is the termination conversation itself. Putting the legalities aside, before firing someone for under-performance or poor behaviours, you must satisfy yourself that you have:

- Demonstrated both to this person and to yourself that you care about them personally by doing your best to understand what is behind under-performance or poor behaviours.
- Given them enough feedback and time to correct their performance.
- Had a career conversation with them where you explored together possible alternative career paths, including the possibility of early termination of employment.

If they have taken no corrective action in the specified time, then you must not delay your termination conversation to avoid discomfort or negative feelings. The more you delay, the more costly it is going to be, both in monetary and emotional terms.

If you need to, discuss your decision to terminate someone's employment contract with a trusted confidante to ensure that it is fair and in the spirit of Radical Candor™. They might provide you with much-needed feedback and support.

Of course, the conversation itself will feel awkward and difficult – to pretend otherwise is unrealistic. However, if the groundwork has been laid properly and the conversation is focused while treating your colleague with dignity and respect, then the message and rationale will be clear – and all parties can move on. The bottom line is that under-performers can harm both performance and culture.

Finally, a few comments on performance and culture. In our experience, under-performance measured by hard KPIs is (obviously) relatively simple to assess. It is more difficult to measure under-performance in the realm of culture. This is where you are observing (and feeling) team disharmony, backbiting, and 'triangle' conversations, and you are receiving subtle (and sometimes not-so-subtle) signals from peers as to the need for action. This is a difficult domain. There is no easy answer; however, in our experience it becomes very clear very quickly if a member of the team is not fit for purpose and action is required.

Of course, one needs to think very carefully about messaging in this space as objective (measurable) performance might be acceptable. It is in situations like these that the team (and the Governing Objective) must take precedence, and the line between diversity of thought and toxicity of fit must be drawn. All our experience tells us that the answer will be obvious, so follow your intuition. The termination process and experience might be painful (and potentially costly), but the long-term benefits outweigh the short-term pain – every time.

Potential Pitfalls

There are a number of pitfalls that must carefully take into consideration:

1. One should be aware that avoiding negative emotions is a huge motivator for delaying termination decisions. We often try and find any excuse to keep the status quo just because we don't want to face our own uncomfortable feelings.

2. Another frequent pitfall is being afraid to admit to yourself or to your boss that you have made a hiring mistake. Unfortunately, hiring mistakes are impossible to avoid even with the best practice principles described in this book.

One very effective way to avoid both pitfalls is to figure out the cost of delaying your decision, which could be very expensive. For example, you should never forget that if anyone on your team is underperforming, then you and your team are underperforming too. Ironically, this could easily trigger your boss to fire you instead.

CONCLUSION

We authored this book on the premise that broadly speaking, most leadership and management books focus either on finding and exploring new fads or are autobiographical in tone.

It was our aim to write a book that stands the test of time and remains at the 'beating heart' of business. We wanted to offer a toolkit that will help leaders create the right frameworks and practices for sustainable value creation. We wanted to develop a way of working around which new concepts, methods, processes, skills, points of view, etc., can be tested or fitted. We wanted to give you, as a leader, a strong foundation for value creation.

Everything in this book is tried and tested in practice – many times over. We have learnt from our mistakes, and have adjusted our approach over the years. Some of our principles and ideas are historically older, while others are new. The common denominator, however, is that they all work.

We hope that what has worked for us will also work for you.

Winging It

As you finish the book and, we hope, have a clear view of how we think a company should be run, we want to share a secret with you.

We have 'winged it' on many occasions.

Nobody can ever escape the fact that sometimes the necessary facts are not available, the timeline is critical, or a decision is needed urgently. The privilege of leadership requires that one must make such decisions, nonetheless. This is where we implore you to listen to your 'gut' and follow your instinct.

However, if your intuition is telling you that either 'it's too good to be true' or 'it doesn't feel right', never ever capitulate to the view of, or pressure from, others. We have done so in the past and lived to regret it. You must have the courage to face down those who might accuse you of dithering, being afraid or not understanding the urgency. Don't ever forget that the buck stops with you. Of course, if it feels right or the downside is limited or setting an example of timely execution is warranted, then by all means 'wing it'.

Notwithstanding the title of this book, 'winging it' does have a place in leadership. It should never be used, however, as the primary instrument in one's leadership toolkit. We would argue that 'winging it' should be the exception, not the norm, so use this book to help you make better decisions, and you won't go far wrong.

END

ACKNOWLEDGEMENTS

We spent much time thinking about this section of the book. Upon reflection, we decided to keep it really short and sweet.

We have been influenced by so many good people (family; friends; work colleagues; members of our community) over our working lives that we didn't want to forget anybody. So, to anyone that we've had the privilege of working for or with, or has spent time listening to us, encouraging us, cajoling us and supporting us, we are forever in your gratitude. We ask that you see this book as a testament to the influence you have had on our values, beliefs and ways of working. We are in your debt.

That said, we wanted to make an exception to the above principle, with a few special mentions. First, to Matt Barrett, Gary Dibb and Peter Herbert from Barclays who introduced us to the concepts of managing for value, and then to Mike Baxter, Dominic Dodd, Mike Jenkins, Ron Langford, Matteo Peccei, Mike Popiel and Matt Symonds, who schooled us in the finer arts. Without all of you, there would be no book. Second, to those dear friends who gave us their time to review the book as it developed – Andrew Carleton, Shane O'Sullivan, Wieke Scholten, Kevin Wall and the aforementioned Matt Symonds and Ron Langford.

Finally, in Jeremy's case, the book is dedicated to a beloved family (Anna, Gabriella, Jack and Lucia). And in Emil's case, to Francesca, Petko, Micky, Emilia and Konstantin whose love is always with him.

GLOSSARY OF TERMS

Balanced Scorecard: A management tool introduced by David Norton that keeps track of the execution of activities and monitors consequences across different stakeholder groups.

Behavioural Segmentation: A marketing segmentation process in which customers are divided into segments by their behaviour patterns that might be useful potential pools of value, e.g., brand loyalty; benefit driven; time/event based.

Behaviours or Company Behaviours: The professional behavioural standards a group should aspire to live by each day and to which they should hold each other accountable.

Career Conversation: The discrete conversation to understand a colleague's motivations and ambitions (based on understanding a life story, dreams, and plans).

CEO: Chief Executive Officer

CFO: Chief Financial Officer

Company Secretariat: Provides administrative support and guidance to company directors.

Competitive Strategy *(See also Participation Strategy):* The set of choices of how to compete in the company's chosen markets.

CSO: Chief Strategy Officer

CTO: Chief Transformation Officer

Customer Value *(See also Value To Customer and Value From Customer):* The value given to and derived from a customer transaction or relationship.

Demographic Segmentation: A marketing segmentation process in which customers or markets are divided into segments by demographic patterns that might be useful potential pools of value, e.g., age; gender; occupation; cultural background; family status.

Dialogue Meetings or Dialogues: Formal strategy and financial planning discussion sessions held as part of the Integrated Planning Process and attended by the business heads/function heads who submit value-based plans to the CEO, CSO, and CFO for debate.

Distribution Channel: The route used by a company to deliver its products or services to its end customers, e.g. wholesale, retail, online, mobile, etc.

Economic Profit (EP) *(See also Economic Value):* A value creation measures suitable for single period measurement; it is not suitable for measuring value creation over multiple reporting periods. It can be used to measure value creation (i.e., economic profitability) per product, per customer segment, per channel, per business unit, etc. It could be both backward- and forward-looking, which means it can be used both for forecasting future performance and managing past performance.

Economic Profit (EP) = 'Earnings After Tax' – 'Cost of Invested Capital'

Alternatively,

EP = ('Return on Equity' – 'Cost of Equity') × 'Invested Equity'

Economic Value (EV) *(See also Economic Profit EP):* A value creation measure to use over multiple reporting periods.

Economic Value (EV) = Invested Equity + Present Value of Future Economic Profit (EP) stream

ESG: It is an all-encompassing acronym for Environmental, Social, and Governance factors. Environmental factors include areas such as climate change, resource depletion, waste, pollution, recycling, deforestation, etc. Social factors include health and safety, working conditions, diversity, human rights, local communities, etc. Finally, governance factors include ethical standards, Board diversity, political lobbying and donations, tax strategy, etc.

Execution Agenda *(See also Management Agenda and Strategy Agenda):* The set of highest-value initiatives/projects pertaining to the delivery of the existing medium-term Financial Plan.

External Performance Measures: Measures reported by the company to the market that enable analysts to make peer comparisons and carry out Extrinsic Valuations. Such measures are not useful for internal strategy development, resource allocation, or business performance management.

Extrinsic Reward *(See also Intrinsic Reward and Total Reward):* Fixed Salary plus Variable Pay plus other financially quantifiable benefits attributable to an employee.

Extrinsic Valuation *(See also Intrinsic Valuation):* The valuation ascribed to a company by external parties, such as analysts based only on the publicly available information about the company. If the company is quoted on the Stock Exchange, such valuation is reflected by the company's share price.

Factbase: The set of facts covering all aspects of a company's Participation and competitive strategy. Producing a factbase of depth and breadth requires deep qualitative and quantitative analysis capabilities.

Fight, Flight, Freeze, and Fawn (4Fs): The set of four possible defence (or coping) mechanisms available to people in any stress-inducing situation.

Financial Plan: The codification of the logical financial implications of the company's strategic choices. It is a multi-year model containing various KPIs, which become Targets of the organisation.

Financial Planning Process: The process that follows from the strategic planning process and which defines the three-to-five years' medium-term Financial Plan (expressed as an income statement and a balance sheet) and a short-term plan (first year), which is also known as the Budget (including a P&L and Cashflow).

Gaming: Playing the strategic and financial planning process when the system is not integrated with many disconnects between the parts.

Governing Objective *(See also Stakeholder Capitalism and Sustainability Tests):* It is the answer to the single most important question in any company:

'Why are we in business in the first place?' It should guide all decisions in the company, including setting the Strategy and the allocation of resources. We argue that the Governing Objective of a shareholder-owned business is to maximise sustainable Owner Value, while the interests of all other stakeholders are seen as input, and not as an output, in the company's strategy.

Group Centre: In large companies this is the organisational unit which sets and maintains the company's policies and standards. Invariably, it is the 'Head Office' comprised of the Board, the executive team, and Specialist/Scale Support Functions.

Integrated Planning Process (IPP): An annual, multi-year process that brings together Strategic and Financial Planning into an integrated cycle.

Internal Performance Measures: Measures used by the company for internal strategy development, resource allocation, and business performance management. Primary measures include Economic Value and Economic Profit.

Intrinsic Reward *(See also Extrinsic Reward and Total Reward):* The reward gained from the presence of an attractive working environment, which could include open and safe communications, a collaborative atmosphere, a competent boss and competent colleagues, available opportunities for learning and development, etc.

Intrinsic Valuation *(See also Extrinsic Valuation):* Management's own internal valuation of the company carried out based on insider knowledge and information.

J-Curve Initiative(s): A single, or portfolio of, investment(s) that requires relatively large initial investment and is not likely to produce an economic return for an extended period of time.

LTIP (Long-Term Incentive Plan): A company scheme rewarding employees for reaching specific targets that lead to increased shareholder value over the long term.

Management Agenda *(See also Strategy Agenda and Execution Agenda):* A document that defines the set of highest-value issues and opportunities facing the company, which must be resolved over the planning horizon for value to be created. It can be divided into Strategy Agenda and Execution Agenda.

Management Model: A rational approach to management that delivers four key elements: Value Goals, Strategy Development, Financial Plan, and Strategy Execution. They are supported and underpinned, in turn, by a fifth element: the company's Organisational Structure.

Managing By Agenda or Agenda Management *(See also Management Agenda):* The process that defines and manages the company's Management Agenda.

Mission *(See also Purpose):* Interchangeable with Purpose – although we prefer 'Purpose' as it carries more of an emotional connotation.

Net Promoter Score®: A Bain & Co customer experience methodology that measures the percentage of customers who are promoters minus the percentage who are detractors. It is an excellent proxy for measuring 'Value To Customers'.

Onboarding: The process by which new hires are integrated into the company.

Operating Manners: Minimum required operating standards for day-to-day working.

Operating Rhythm: The set of interdependent cyclical processes as explicitly defined by management.

Organisational Blueprint: A codified document that sets boundaries and the processes for how a company should be led and managed (underpinned by Governing Objective, Vision, and Management Model).

Organisational Culture: A set of shared basic values, beliefs, behaviours, Operating Manners, processes, etc., which the company's employees use on a daily basis.

Organisational Structure: Organisational Structure refers to the hierarchical arrangement of lines of authority, communications, rights, and duties within an organisation. It determines how roles, power, and responsibilities are assigned and how information flows between different levels of management.

Participation Strategy *(See also Competitive Strategy):* It is the set of choices of which markets to compete in. Participation and Competitive choices together define a company's Strategy.

Performance Management: The process that holds colleagues to account for both delivery of commitments and associated Behaviours.

Psychological Safety: Concept defined by Amy Edmondson as 'a shared belief held by members of a team that the team is safe for interpersonal risk taking'; that is, the work environment they operate in feels safe, so they don't have to limit their self-expression or censor what they say or do because of a fear of being punished; an environment that encourages, recognises, and rewards individuals for their contribution.

Purpose *(See also Vision):* The reason for being, or the 'raison d'être', of the company. It is usually a statement that has the potential to ignite people's intrinsic motivation to be a part of something bigger than themselves. We like to think of it as a part of a broader company Vision.

Radical Candor™: The tools and techniques defined by Kim Scott in the book *Radical Candor*. The core principle is to care personally and to challenge directly.

Recognition: The timely acknowledgement of actions or work that brings value to the company.

Risk Appetite: The level of risk that the company is prepared to accept in pursuit of its Governing Objective before action is required to reduce the risk.

Scale Support Functions: The organisational units that provide both specialist services and economies of scale/scope for the SBUs.

Selection and Recruitment: The process through which management identifies a set of potential candidates for vacant roles and selects preferred candidates.

Glossary

Service Level Agreement (SLA): A commitment between a service provider and customer, usually based on quality, quantity, availability, roles, and responsibilities.

Specialist Support Functions: The organisational units that provide specialist services for the Strategic Business Units, e.g. Strategy & Planning, Corporate Development, Legal, Procurement, Tax, etc.

Stakeholder Capitalism: The idea that corporations should serve and balance the interests of all stakeholders, and not just the shareholders, i.e. the interests of all stakeholders are seen as input into the company's strategy.

Strategic Business Unit (SBU): The main value-creating organisational unit in any company. It can have various dimensions such as Product/Service Market, Customer Segment, Distribution Channel, or Geography. There must always be a primary dimension to an SBU to ensure management accountability is defined beyond doubt. Such primary dimensions must always be driven by Strategy.

Strategic Planning Process: The process which defines the long-term strategy of the company, and which aims to maximise sustainable value subject to a series of Sustainability Tests.

Strategy & Planning Team: A Specialist Support Function reporting to the CSO that defines and executes a company's Integrated Planning Process and owns (and delivers) the Strategy Agenda. It requires a mix of deep quantitative and qualitative capabilities and experience.

Strategy Agenda *(See also Management Agenda and Execution Agenda)*: The set of highest-value issues and opportunities pertaining to the company's strategy arising from the factbase insights which have not yet been grounded in the Financial Plan. One can also think of the Strategy Agenda as the research and development agenda for where future value could be created or destroyed.

Strategy Development Process: The process that develops an explicit articulation of the market and competitive choices made by the company at any point in time. That is, it is the process through which the company's leadership becomes clear on which markets they have chosen to participate in and how they have chosen to compete in those markets.

Leading Without Winging It

Strategy Execution: The 'what/how/who/why' of delivery of the medium-term Financial Plan and the Execution Agenda.

Sustainability Test(s) *(See also Governing Objective, ESG, and Stakeholder Capitalism):* A set of input constraints (or Decision Rules) to ensure that value created for the company owners is sustained over the long term and does not come at the expense of customers, colleagues, the community, or destruction of the environment. In other words, considerations for these stakeholders become an input rather than an output to strategy development and implementation.

Targets or Performance Targets *(See also Value Goals):* Targets are the outcome of the strategic and Financial Plan in the form of specific, time-bound deliverables which are to be performance managed. These are not the same as Goals.

Targets or Performance Targets *(See also Value Goals):* Specific and concrete commitments which are used to measure progress towards the Goals. Unlike Goals, Targets are typically shorter-term deliverables, which are the output of the Strategy Development Process, rather than an input.

Three Lines of Defence Model: This is a risk management framework used primarily in banking which divides responsibility risk management across three functions (or three lines of defence). First line of defence is represented by the owners and managers of key risks, processes, and controls. Second line of defence is represented by overseers of key risks, processes, and controls, usually known as Risk and Compliance function. Third line of defence is represented by the providers of independent risk assurance to key risks, processes, and controls, usually known as Group Internal Audit.

Total Reward *(See also Extrinsic Reward and Total Reward):* The sum of Intrinsic Reward, Extrinsic Reward, and Recognition.

Total Shareholder Return (TSR): A market-based measure for retrospective value creation that can be readily calculated from Stock Exchange data. It is calculated as:

$$TSR = Share\ Price\ Appreciation + Dividend\ Yield\ over\ the\ same\ period$$

TSR is ideal for performance management purposes, such as corporate Long-Term Incentive Plans (LTIPs).

Value From Customer *(See also Value To Customer and Customer Value):* The price that the company charges the customer for its product/service minus the company's total economic cost to serve this product/service.

Value Goals or Goals *(See also Targets):* The rational, stretching but realistic, and quantitative aspirations for the company. They are always an input to strategy development and are not the same as Targets.

Value Narrative or Value Story: This is the leadership narrative which articulates how the company intends to create sustainable value for its owners/investors over time. It communicates clearly and compellingly the long-term strategy of the company in both non-financial and financial terms.

Value To Customer *(See also Value From Customer and Customer Value):* The benefits and the satisfaction which customers derive from a product/service minus the price they have paid for this product/service.

Values or Company Values: Ways of being or the inner qualities shared by people working in the company.

Vision *(See also Purpose, Values, Behaviours, Operating Manners, and Management Model):* Vision is defined as the combination of the organisation's Purpose, Values, Behaviours, and Operating Manners, which in partnership with a rational Management Model, is a key enabler of delivering the Governing Objective.

WHO Focused Interview® *(See also WHO®):* An interview that tests the short-list of candidates for fit against the outcomes and competencies described in the Scorecard.

WHO Reference Interview® *(See also WHO®):* An interview with referees that delves deeply into the candidate's historic, strengths, and rating, and probes the underlying context.

WHO Scorecard® *(See also WHO®):* A document that describes exactly what a person is required to accomplish in a role; based on outcomes and competencies that describe a job well done.

WHO Screening Interview® *(See also WHO®):* An interview that screens the long list of potential candidates using prescribed questions.

WHO Top-Grading Interview® *(See also WHO®):* A chronological interview that tests the short-list of candidates for 'A-player' rating.

WHO®: The tools and techniques defined by Geoff Smart and Randy Street in their book *Who: The A Method for Hiring.* The core principle is to use the WHO methodology to source and select 'A-players'.

AUTHORS' BIOGRAPHIES

Jeremy Masding

LinkedIn Profile: www.linkedin.com/in/jeremymasding

Jeremy left school at 18 and over the next 40 years, built a career through combining learning by doing, taking challenging roles, investing in education, and delivering results. By observing many different definitions of leadership, involving both good and bad practices, Jeremy went from cashier to CEO and, along the way, developed a leadership framework that could be applied successfully across a wide variety of roles and businesses. It is this framework, which evolved and strengthened in partnership with Emil over nearly 25 years of working together, that underpins the book. The framework offers a clear, practical, and actionable approach to help leaders of all experience levels be the best they can be.

Jeremy most recently used the framework when brought in to rescue Permanent TSB PLC, one of Ireland's biggest banks, which was nationalised in 2011 during the banking crisis. According to one newspaper "[Masding] inherited one of Europe's worst banks when taking the job in 2012. The Welshman somehow managed to keep the show on the road… [and] saved an institution from collapse."

Jeremy is an Associate and Fellow of the Chartered Institute of Bankers, a Certified Bank Director and holds an MBA from Manchester Business School.

Emil Ivanov

LinkedIn Profile: www.linkedin.com/in/emilivanov

Emil is an experienced business leader with a strong background in the financial services industry. Emil's expertise covers strategy, planning, change management, and investor relations. Emil is recognised for outstanding leadership abilities, strong analytical skills, and attention to detail. Emil is also known for an ability to build and inspire high-performing teams, achieving exceptional results. Emil has always been driven by the deep desire to understand the inner workings of business, leading, managing, and the dynamics of interacting with people.

Emil's partnership with Jeremy in writing this book has been driven by a simple mission: to share our learnings and experiences in the simplest of terms – the key leadership issues, the principles to be applied in solving the issues, the positive actions that can be taken towards that end, and the pitfalls to be avoided.

Emil is fascinated by why people do what they do, especially if it does not serve them or their company positively in the long-term. As a keen student of human behaviour Emil's aim is to inspire others to push past their limitations and, pursue personal and professional growth.

Emil holds an MBA from INSEAD and a bachelor's degree from the American University in Bulgaria. Emil is also a Fellow of the Association of Chartered Certified Accountants.

GETTING IN TOUCH

You can access further resources at our website:

www.leadingwithoutwingingit.com

On the website, we have provided our contact details, and would be delighted to expand on any aspect covered in this book if it would be of help to you or your organisation.

As we mentioned in the Introduction, we toyed between going deep on a few topics or staying broad. After much debate, we decided on the latter: to offer an integrated, rational and emotional toolkit for leading a business and maximising value. Throughout the book we were focussed on supplying the reader with a set of tools and principles that either individually or collectively would support better leadership.

Leading Without Winging It

Milton Keynes UK
Ingram Content Group UK Ltd.
UKHW020917220424
441551UK00017B/1205